IT Mismanagement Patterns

Michael Vartanyan
Vasily Kuznetsov

Send us your feedback and your patterns to
patterns@mismanagement.it

Copyright ©2020 by Michael Vartanyan and Vasily Kuznetsov.
All rights reserved.
Illustrations and cover: Vasily Kuznetsov, Natalya Volkova
Editor: Donna Cole
Published via Amazon KDP.
ISBN: 9781729310519

Contents

Contents   ii

Introduction   1

Patterns   5
     Activity imitation 5
     Analysis Paralysis 8
     Apple from the tree 10
     Architectural answering machine 12
     Assertion of culture 14
     Beam in the eye fallacy 16
     Business case fabrication 18
     Business case protectionism 20
     Buy before you think 22
     Cargo cult standard compliance 24
     Cast iron triangle 26
     Circular decision 28
     Common malpractice 30
     Concealed consensus 32
     Confirmation-biased reporting 34
     Cost sink 36
     Critical dependency on imaginary assets 37
     Cutting the wrong corners 38
     Deadline-driven estimation 40
     Death march 41
     Depreciation of commitment 43

Disposable leader 45
Doing other things 47
Doomed to success 49
Einbahnstrasse 51
Enterprise technology 53
Escalation of commitment 55
Every change is sacred 57
Face transition 59
Fake training 60
Faking ends meet 62
Global zero 63
God mode 65
Goodbye party 67
Guardian angels 69
Guilt-based management 71
Highlander principle 73
Holy cow project 75
Holy rodeo 77
Hope based estimation 78
Imaginary superpower 80
Irrational unified process (a.k.a. Avalanche model) . 81
Late awakening 83
Local hero 85
Lock, stock and barrel 87
Lock-in discount 89
Looking into the future 91
Management by hysteria 93
Manager in absentia 95
Manager-in-the-middle attack 97
Manualisation 99
McClane effect 100
News improvement 102
Pareto denial 104
Potemkin standard compliance 106
Primacy of principles 108
Publicity-based valuation 110

Pusher (a.k.a. Loyal facade) 112
Quantity assurance 114
Quick fix of doom 115
Responsibility delegation 117
Responsibility escalation 119
Responsibility outsourcing 121
Reverse business justification 123
Reverse requirements gathering 125
Risk of programming 127
Robin Hood financial management 129
Runaway interdependence 131
Scale of economies 133
Scope drain 135
Shadow governance 137
Silence of the maltreated minds 139
Split personality order 141
Strategy laundering 143
Strategy outsourcing 145
Submission to urgency 147
Suboptimal improvement 149
Tainted knowledge 151
Troglodyte manager 153
Turn into hedgehogs 155
Umph 157
Unbribe 159
Virtual support contract 161
Write-only document 163
Wunderwaffe project 165

Categories 167
  Business justification 168
  Clear roles and responsibilities 173
  Communication 177
  Decision-making 179
  Documentation and reporting 183
  Fact-based environment 187

    People 190
    Planning 194
    Recruitment 198
    Quality 203

Bibliography   207

Introduction

Your project is approved — congratulations, dear project manager! Sure, you didn't get all the money you asked for. You value transparency, so you were open to your management about your reserves and risk budgets. Management didn't find these necessary. They also took the side of developers in their fight with the marketing people over one of the features. Marketing said that the feature is essential for sales; the developers argued that the product will easily work without it. Your bosses told you that they understand the complexity of your work, so they are taking this feature out of the scope to reduce complexity ... and budget. The project is simpler and cheaper now — thanks to your management's goodwill — so full delivery by a mandatory deadline is now seen as a given.

So here we go. Your budget, time, and scope are all fixed and sealed. Then something unexpected happens, and you need to put out a fire. Can you spend a bit more on that fire? No, the budget is fixed. Can you take a bit of additional time or take out some features? You can try — if you want to see your CEO break a promise they made personally to the company's biggest client. The only thing you *can* do is reduce quality, a parameter dearest to the perfectionist now dying inside of you.

Sounds familiar? Indeed, it happens even in organisations that like to brag about their mature management practices. We call it the **cast iron triangle**, a situation where all of the components of the "triple constraint" or the project management triangle, are fixed and immovable no matter what. The cast iron triangle is not the only way to mismanage. In fact, we have identified dozens of patterns that are practised in IT mismanagement. The goal of this book is to name these and provide ways to identify them. This will equip you with ways to understand what might be going wrong at your workplace and the terminology to discuss it with your colleagues.

We have taken an engineering perspective and approach to the analysis of problems and situations. It is a good approach, but there are few management books that look at things from this angle. We have been careful with providing recommendations, and when we do we provide them in a language that both engineers and management will find familiar. Engineers are often correct in suggesting the course of action to managers but find it difficult to woo them. If you are analysing why your boss rejects or ignores your perfectly reasonable and right suggestions (you should be!) this book will feed your analysis with insights about the thoughts that constantly occupy the typical manager's mind and very rarely happen to cross the engineer's one.

There are 85 patterns in this book. Each pattern has a name we hope will become a common term: readers of this book will then know what to call "this" when they see it. The patterns describe situations that would make a sane professional want to cry, so we have tried to speak about them in a way to make you smile instead. Even when cynical, a smile is a positive reaction, and a positive attitude is a good starting point for making things better.

Each pattern falls into one or more categories. If you are reading this book in print, the Categories section is available on page 167. If you are reading online or in PDF, the category names are hyperlinked to their descriptions. Finally, some patterns are usually seen together, cause each other, or are otherwise related. In a few cases, the relationship is strong enough that the name of one pattern is mentioned in the description of another. More often, however, related patterns are listed separately with an explanation of the relationship.

Cast iron triangle

A situation where all vertices of the project management triangle (budget, schedule, and scope) are fixed by powers far above the project manager's pay grade. Faced with reality, the only remaining parameter that the project manager is at freedom to influence — negatively — is quality. An additional negative effect of a cast iron triangle is on the morale of the team, who are powerless to fix the project but are often, nevertheless, held liable for the suboptimal outcome.

Category

- Decision-making
- Communication

Related patterns

- Arguably, the most negotiable of the constraints at the beginning of the project is time. **Deadline-driven estimation** immobilises the time constraint, closing the cast iron triangle on a project that would otherwise be doable.

- If the cast iron triangle is not addressed early in the project, the whole undertaking has a very good chance of turning into a **death march** or ending in an **umph**.

- It takes a strong work ethic from a project manager who finds themselves inside the cast iron triangle not to start **cutting the wrong corners**.

In concluding this introduction, let us once again point out the goals (and non-goals) of this book. Our main goal is to enable the reader to recognise problematic patterns, not fix them. We firmly believe that there are no universal solutions or right answers in management, for it is not an exact science. What will work for you in fixing the problems will depend on who you are as a person, where you are in the organisation, what the organisation's culture is like, and many other factors.

"Don't do any of the things we describe" is not a valid recommendation: some negative patterns, such as cargo cult standard compliance, have their place in certain situations as much as positive ones. However, whatever you do, remember that complexity is inevitable in an organisation of human beings. To act, you need to understand the entire landscape around you, down to the tiny details that may have an unexpectedly strong influence. Our humble hope is that this book will advance this understanding and provide you with tools and terminology to discuss it with your colleagues and bosses.

Patterns

Activity imitation

Performing work that is related to a project but doesn't lead to achieving its goals.

Activity imitation can be done on purpose or inadvertently. For example, in any nontrivial undertaking, starting the work without a reasonably detailed plan can easily result in accidental activity imitation; as can development of architecture without detailed understanding of the requirements and technologies involved.

Activity imitation is not specific to project work, and it occurs even more often in operations. With few exceptions, projects are planned to change the *status quo* and are measured by whether something positive promised actually happens. Operations, in turn,

IT Mismanagement Patterns

should maintain the *status quo* and are measured by whether they have prevented anything negative from happening. It is inherently difficult to produce evidence of a non-event[1] and even more difficult to analyse the reasons this non-event does not occur. It is therefore much harder to differentiate justified operational activity from activity imitation.

Project management methodologies provide recommendations for making sure all the work done within a project contributes to its goals. Almost any standard methodology for organising operations will also have guidance on avoiding activity imitation. TPS[2] and Lean[3] methodologies contain specific guidance on eliminating muda[4], and activity imitation can certainly be considered a type of muda.

Categories

- Business justification

Related patterns

- In cases of intentional activity imitation, the source of decisions is often concealed using **circular decision** techniques or **responsibility outsourcing**.

- It is possible to turn activity imitation into justified work *ex-post* by adjusting the goals of the project via **reverse requirements gathering**.

- One of the possible reasons for intentional activity imitation is **news improvement**: the project appears to have pro-

---

[1] *"Reports that say that something hasn't happened are always interesting to me,"* ex US Defense Secretary Donald Rumsfeld during a Pentagon news briefing in February 2002
[2] http://en.wikipedia.org/wiki/Toyota_Production_System
[3] http://en.wikipedia.org/wiki/Lean_manufacturing
[4] http://en.wikipedia.org/wiki/Muda_(Japanese_term)

gressed even though it is not actually closer to achieving its objectives.

- Activity imitation is bound to happen when **every change is sacred**.

- Training activities are highly visible across the organisation and are usually seen in a positive light by everyone, so activity can be imitated splendidly by investing in **fake training**.

- When thinking presents a challenge, you can **buy before you think** for others to see that you are doing something.

IT Mismanagement Patterns

Analysis Paralysis

Spending a disproportionate amount of time in the planning phase and not committing to any decision or action until it's too late.

This very general pattern hurts IT projects more than others, as IT projects can adjust a working product rather cheaply compared to, for example, projects in the construction industry or automotive engineering. Proofs of concept and prototypes are indispensable tools for shaping the direction of a project. Starting with a small system and growing it in response to users' demands works very well in IT, so over-analysing is even less practical here than in other pursuits.

Plans are not supposed to be perfect predictions of the future, and even the best of them will need adjustments as the team learns new information. At some point in the project, the plan gets to a state where polishing it further adds less value than starting the implementation. It is hard to pinpoint this moment exactly, but it grows easier to recognise that you have passed it as you move further beyond.

Categories

- Decision-making
- Planning

- Business justification

Related patterns

- Excessive analysing without decisions or actions is a form of **activity imitation**.
- If the time has almost run out and you're still analysing, trying to save the project and deliver the product might turn it into a **death march**.
- Lots of thinking without sufficient information might still not produce a realistic plan and might result in **hope based** or worse **deadline-driven estimates**.
- **Critical dependencies on imaginary assets** and other practical considerations often surface after you've started implementation, so they will be noticed later if the analysis phase lasts too long.

IT Mismanagement Patterns

Apple from the tree [5]

The tendency of unprofessional or incompetent managers to hire employees with similar characteristics for the convenience of collusion, or because of the inability to judge the competence of others in an area they do not understand.

The result of this pattern sets the organisation on a slippery slope of becoming less competent and more corrupt. The unfairness of the situation can also decrease the motivation of competent employees. Nurture a fact-based environment in your organisation to avoid development of this pattern. Protect your internal whistle-blowers and remember that the worst mistake a manager can make is the hiring mistake.

Category

- Recruitment

---

[5] See http://en.wiktionary.org/wiki/apple_does_not_fall_far_from_the_tree

Related patterns

- The **silence of the maltreated minds** is what happens if management fails to take action or is otherwise perceived as condoning incompetence and corruption.

- **Concealed consensus** and other forms of responsibility avoidance are easier in a management structure consisting of insecure and uncritical individuals.

- Apple from the tree hires intended for increasing the sense of control often become vehicles of a **manager-in-the-middle attack**.

IT Mismanagement Patterns

Architectural answering machine

An architect giving the same guidance on the choice of technology and approach for any project without consideration of requirements, fitness for purpose, pre-existing solutions, time and resource constraints.

This might seem justified on the grounds of producing uniform and consistent architecture, but that would be putting the cart before the horse. As beautiful as it might be, the architecture is not very valuable if it stands in the way of achieving results. Make sure that architecture departments are aware that they exist solely to help the organisation achieve its business goals, while solid architecture by itself cannot be a business goal.

Category

- Fact-based environment

- Business justification

Related patterns

- The **Highlander principle** and **management by hysteria** are some of the common causes of the architectural answering machine pattern.

- **Reverse requirements gathering** could be used to make the predetermined choice of technology seem more appropriate.

- As architectural answering machines fail to provide the adequate architectural guidance needed for organisations to realise their business goals, they create a power vacuum that can lead to creating or reinforcing already existing **shadow governance**.

- Architectural answering machines, in their inherent disconnect with reality, are also highly susceptible to giving **turn into hedgehogs** type advice and introducing **critical dependencies on imaginary assets**.

IT Mismanagement Patterns

Assertion of culture

A staff member's persistent unwillingness to behave in a manner consistent or at least compatible with the organisation's culture, while claiming said culture to be wrong and needing radical, momentary change. The assertion of culture typically leads to isolation of the staff member by the majority, staff grievances, and reduction of overall efficiency within the area of influence. It is common among managers hired from another organisation or industry branch who are struggling to perceive and analyse the new reality around them. A pre-recruitment briefing about existing culture and screening of potential cultural fitness[6] of the candidate may reduce the likelihood of this happening, but the organisation must be prepared to tackle instances promptly and decisively.

---

[6] One doesn't need to fully comply to fit. Indeed, some recruitment drives have *influencing* the existing culture as their primary purpose. But in order to influence without being alienated, one needs to fit in first.

Category

- Communication
- Recruitment

Related patterns

- The assertion of culture on the part of newly-hired management frequently leads to **split personality order**.

- A **troglodyte manager** is one of the possible outcomes of an unsuccessful assertion of culture.

- The assertion of culture can be greatly reinforced by combining it with the **apple from the tree** pattern.

- If you fail to assert your culture try to form a **shadow governance** instead.

IT Mismanagement Patterns

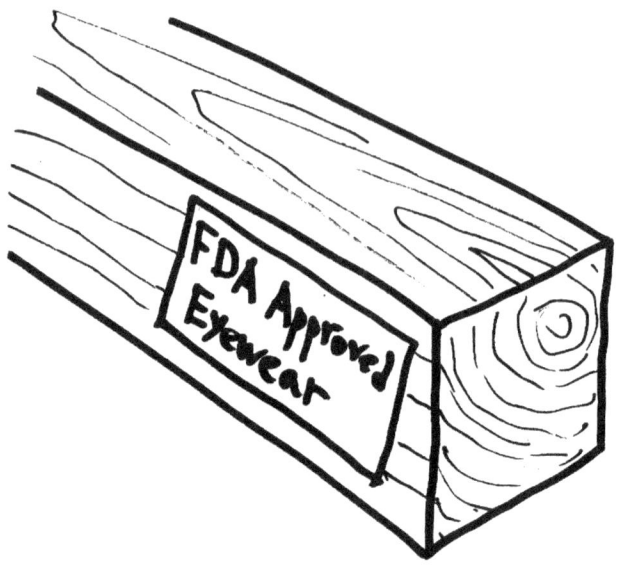

Beam in the eye[7] fallacy

Pointing out small flaws, typically of a paperwork kind, such as with process organisation or standards compliance, while ignoring much more serious problems in another area. Beam in the eye fallacy usually happens because the other area is a **holy cow project** or the team working in that area is more loyal to the party line[8]. Calling people out on such behaviour can be problematic as it can be counter-argued as a "red herring": something that is currently not the point of discussion[9]. A reasonable alternative could be to consistently and continuously make a point about prioritisation of concerns and insist that concerns across the board are tackled according to their priority.

---

[7] Matthew 7:3 [20]
[8] See http://en.wikipedia.org/wiki/Party_line_(politics)
[9] More about this exotic fish: https://en.wikipedia.org/wiki/Red_herring

Category

- Decision-making

Other related patterns

- **Apple from the tree** can lead to favouritism that results in the beam in the eye fallacy.

- Some victims of the beam in the eye fallacy may become convinced to prioritise formal compliance over substantive results, embarking on the road to becoming **global zeros**.

IT Mismanagement Patterns

Business case fabrication

Artificially creating a business case for a project by implementing unneeded (sometimes harmful) changes to alter the baseline, and hide some part of the cost, effort or risk so that the project starts to look worthy of investment. A more robust baseline analysis method and practice[10] will make it harder for project proponents to apply business case fabrication.

Category

- Business justification

Related patterns

- **Business case protectionism** is a related pattern. The difference mostly regards timing: fabrication happens before and during project initiation, but protectionism takes place during its main phase.

---

[10] Sometimes it helps to just ask whether the goal can be achieved by undoing something that had been done recently rather than doing something new.

- Various forms of **concealed consensus** can be used to hide the source of the decisions that lead to business case fabrication and make them appear rational.

- **Holy cow projects** can be seen as an example of business case fabrication solely by asserting the extreme importance of the project. Once such a project is established, further activities can be added to it, thus automatically acquiring a business case (see **holy rodeo**).

- **Every change is sacred** rhetoric is typically used to justify unnecessary and harmful changes implemented to fabricate a business case.

IT Mismanagement Patterns

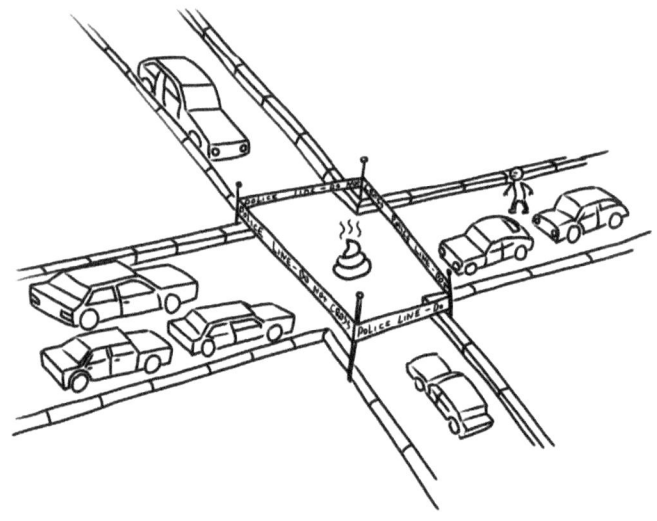

Business case protectionism

*Disallowing useful and justified activity on the grounds it will deliver some benefit that is supposed to be delivered by an ongoing or planned **holy cow project**.*

Management often uses scorched earth tactics toward anything that is playing in the same field with their holy cow, so the said cow can maintain at least some impression of business justification.

Category

- Business justification

Other related patterns

- **Business case fabrication** is a related pattern and these two often appear together.

- Various forms of **concealed consensus** make business case protectionism harder to identify and challenge.

- **News improvement** can be used to make competing activity look less practical, as the problems it is supposed to solve are "just about" to be solved by the protected project.

Buy before you think

Buying commercial IT solutions without careful analysis of requirements or consideration of other options (e.g. using free software or custom development).

Often the leading motives for buy before you think are **responsibility outsourcing** and avoiding the **risk of programming**; it may also be a result of vendors' predatory sales tactics toward incompetent decision-makers.

Well-designed procurement rules and a reasonably militant procurement department are sometimes able to protect the organisation from thoughtless purchases. The real solution, however, is to "think before you buy."

Category

- Decision-making

Other related patterns

- Acquiring software that is unnecessary -- or impossible to use — could be a form of **activity imitation**.

- Buy before you think is an example of thinking dominated by **primacy of principles** and it frequently leads to **suboptimal improvements**.

- When compelled to demonstrate thinking behind the decision to buy, decision-makers usually resort to demonstrating that their purchase features all of the **lock, stock and barrel**.

IT Mismanagement Patterns

Cargo cult[11] standard compliance

Following the standard formally without understanding the logic behind it, in the hope that by going through all the prescribed steps and producing all the prescribed documents, the result will be improved. This is known to work at least partially and to be particularly effective if applied by less competent staff; however, it is still an anti-pattern for a healthy organisation. Even when it provides some benefits, cargo cult standard compliance is less efficient than when standard followers understand the logic and motivation behind the standard as well the boundaries of its applicability. Situations when a broken cargo cult standard replaces something non-standard but working are also not uncommon; in such cases, cargo cultism is clearly harmful.

Category

- Fact-based environment

Related patterns

- Simple cargo cultists are the way they are because they do not know any better. **Potemkin standard compliance** is a deliberately deceptive cousin of this pattern.

---

[11]See https://en.wikipedia.org/wiki/Cargo_cult for the origin of the term "cargo cult".

- As cargo cultists don't understand the logic behind the steps they are following, they might spend an unreasonable amount of time trying to perfect things that are not worth it, leading to **activity imitation**.

IT Mismanagement Patterns

Cast iron[12] triangle

A situation where all vertices of the project management triangle (budget, schedule, and scope) are fixed by powers far above the project manager's pay grade. Faced with reality, the only remaining parameter that the project manager is at freedom to influence — negatively — is quality. An additional negative effect of a cast iron triangle is on the morale of the team, who are powerless to fix the project but are often, nevertheless, held liable for the suboptimal outcome.

Category

- Decision-making
- Communication

---

[12] We had to change the metal in the name of this pattern to make it distinguishable from one describing the "iron triangle", a by no means less optimal way the US legislature functions. For more details on the latter, see https://en.wikipedia.org/wiki/Iron_triangle_(US_politics)

Related patterns

- Arguably, the most negotiable of the constraints at the beginning of the project is time. **Deadline-driven estimation** immobilises the time constraint, closing the cast iron triangle on a project that would otherwise be doable.

- If the cast iron triangle is not addressed early in the project, the whole undertaking has a very good chance of turning into a **death march** or ending in an **umph**.

- It takes a strong work ethic from a project manager who finds themselves inside the cast iron triangle not to start **cutting the wrong corners**.

IT Mismanagement Patterns

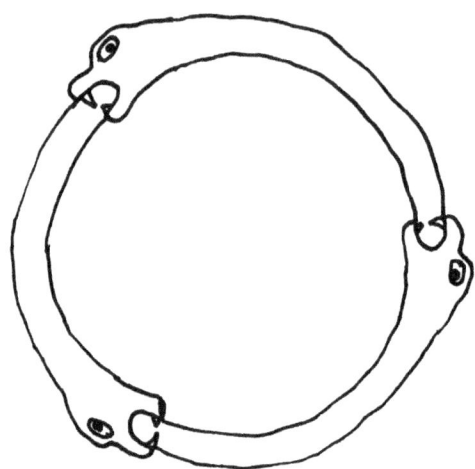

Circular decision

A decision that is taken by a group of people where any individual member of the group, when asked about the justification of the decision, points to another member or members. Circular decisions can result from misunderstanding, groupthink[13], or malicious collusion.

Having the proponent's name[14] on record for any significant decision helps to avoid less successful decisions becoming circular when it comes to explaining why things went wrong.

---

[13]See https://en.wikipedia.org/wiki/Groupthink

[14]In our opinion, decision-making by committee should generally be avoided. If there is no way around this, there are myriads of documented ways to make it more effective. In any case, managers who are accountable for the final decision of the committee should be extra careful when no member of the committee is prepared to sign for the entirety of the substantive justification for the decision without referring to any fellow committee members' names.

Category

- Decision-making
- Clear roles and responsibilities

Related patterns

- **Concealed consensus** is a malicious form of circular decision that is taken, in reality, by consensus of all parties.
- **Responsibility escalation** is involving supervisors in a circular decision to place the responsibility with them.
- **Responsibility outsourcing** can take a form of involving external organisations or consultants in a circular decision to place the responsibility with them.

IT Mismanagement Patterns

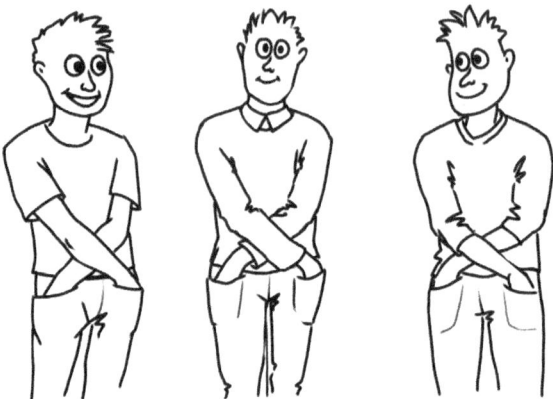

Common malpractice

A clearly inefficient and sometimes ineffective process that could be hugely improved by application of well-known, easy, quick and inexpensive fixes. This process is often kept in place for bogus reasons such as awaiting completion of a **wunderwaffe project**, incompatibility of fixes with **looking into the future**, etc.

Category

- Business justification

Other related patterns

- In entrenched **apple from the tree** structures, a review of processes is particularly unwelcome as it invariably questions the need for jobs occupied by those not contributing.
- Common malpractice is a form of **Pareto denial**.

- **Troglodyte managers** isolate themselves from negative feedback about existing common malpractices and may honestly perceive them as effective ones.

IT Mismanagement Patterns

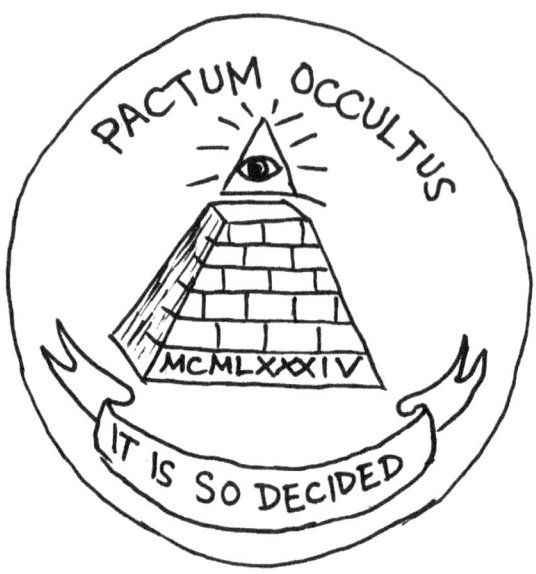

Concealed consensus

Concealing the source of a decision taken consensually by a group of people where each member of the group pretends that they didn't have the leading role in the decision-making or were forced to agree by the rest of the group. Concealed consensus is a general-purpose responsibility avoidance tool that can be used to protect the culprit when implementing many of the harmful patterns in this book.

Category

- Clear roles and responsibilities

Related patterns

- Concealed consensus is a culpable form of **circular decision** and guidance to avoid those also applies here.

IT Mismanagement Patterns

Confirmation-biased reporting

Reporting only facts that prove the desired version of reality while ignoring evidence to the contrary. As confirmation bias is hard to avoid, most people engage in "honest" confirmation-biased reporting even when they don't realise it. Some people augment natural confirmation bias with additional cherry-picking of facts to make their opinion more convincing, thus treading dangerously close to true **news improvement**.

Category

- Fact-based environment

Other related patterns

- When using a **lock, stock and barrel** approach, people tend to overestimate the rate of completion of the project, seeing the out-of-the-box 80% delivered as 80% of the work done.

They forget (or omit) that the remaining 20% that are also critical for overall success contain most of the complexity.

- This pattern affects **troglodyte managers** more as they don't have an opportunity to correct their biases by talking to other people.

- Confirmation-biased reporting can be used as a method of **business case fabrication**, for instance by exaggerating the scale of a problem.

IT Mismanagement Patterns

Cost sink

An activity that is wasting money but is nevertheless continued to avoid declaring past investment completely lost.

Cost sink can be seen as the site of repeated application of the sunk cost fallacy[15]. Sufficiently granular financial management, portfolio performance reviews, and a certain amount of goodwill can easily identify cost sinks for elimination.

Category

- Business justification

Related patterns

- **Escalation of commitment** is a similar pattern, with the focus on reputational rather than financial damage.

---

[15] See https://en.wikipedia.org/wiki/Sunk_costs

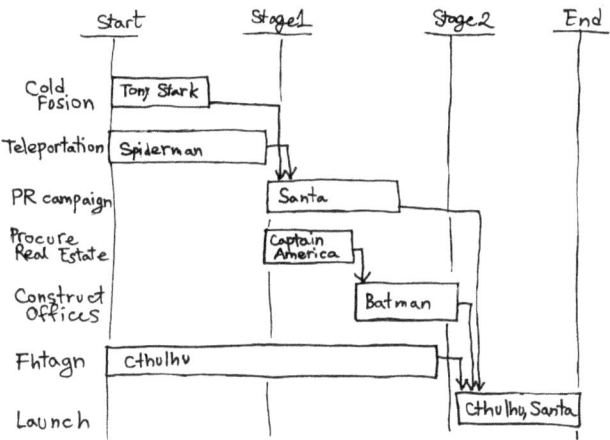

Critical dependency on imaginary assets

Dependency on an unavailable but sought skill — or an inexistent but planned component — which slips into a project without proper consideration of the risk that the dependency will not be available when needed.

Category

- Planning

Related patterns

- **Hope based estimation** is a related pattern that can be fuelled by imaginary assets required for this project and produce imaginary dependencies for other projects.

IT Mismanagement Patterns

Cutting the wrong corners

Accelerating visible, immediate progress in a way that ultimately results in a more expensive and longer road to the final goal.

Taking on excessive and unnecessary technological debt is one common example of cutting the wrong corners.

Category

- Business justification
- Decision-making

Related patterns

- Cutting the wrong corners is an obvious way of **activity imitation** in response to a mandate to accelerate delivery or meet an impossible deadline.

- Cutting the wrong corners allows intermediate milestones to be achieved more quickly and can be a tool for **news improvement**.

IT Mismanagement Patterns

Deadline-driven estimation

Massaging the estimates to fit an externally-imposed deadline or just using the time and resources available as a grand total estimate without looking into details of the work.

Deadline-driven estimation works well with **hope based estimation**.

Category

- Planning

Related patterns

- Deadline-driven estimation is one example of a **doomed to success** way of thinking.
- Asking subordinates for effort estimates while asserting that the work must be completed before a certain deadline is a clever method of **responsibility delegation**.

Patterns

Death march[16]

A project that has little chance of success, but is actively funded and supported by management. The death march is typically the final stage of an unlucky **holy cow project**. Staff caught in a death march usually understand the grim situation, but often continue the work (fuelling **activity imitation**) out of fear of superiors and/or with the hope for some form of compensation. Management tools used during a death march typically include excessive overtime, **cutting the wrong corners** and reshuffling the project team to take advantage of **depreciation of commitment**.

Category

- Planning
- Business justification

---

[16]This term, of military origin, was popularised as a project management concept in a namesake book by Edward Yourdon.

Related patterns

- Believing that the project is **doomed to success** is a good indication that it might be a death march. It's also a good mental aid if you have to keep on marching.

Patterns

Depreciation of commitment

The gradual decline of the significance of commitments and decisions as the people involved are moved to other projects or leave the organisation. Depreciation of commitment is capable of silencing important management feedback about goals not reached and methods that have not been working for years. The documentation of commitments and decisions with their respective expected value and diligent benefits reviews help avoid depreciation of commitment.

Category

- Documentation and reporting

Related patterns

- Depreciation of commitment is one of the chief tools in achieving **scope drain**.

IT Mismanagement Patterns

- You can eliminate many commitments by firing a **disposable leader**.

Patterns

Disposable leader

A manager hired for the purpose of **responsibility outsourcing** *with regard to a particular major decision or strategy choice, typically in the beginning of the new* **hysteria-based management** *cycle.*

Often disposable leaders will be introduced as a "transformational leader" or "change evangelist". After the hysteria collapses, all blame can be put on the disposable leader, who, at this point, is usually conveniently no longer around. The obvious advice here is to not do it, at least not more than once to the same people, or the trust will be very hard to repair.

Category

- People

45

Other related patterns

- **Pushers** — once they are done (or have failed) — are disposable.

- If you pull a disposable leader on your collective a couple of times, then the **silence of the maltreated minds** is virtually guaranteed.

- A **goodbye party** is a related pattern, although it can also be thrown by non-disposable managers. In case of a disposable leader, their whole tenure in the organisation is essentially one big goodbye party.

Doing other things

Stopping the work on an unfinished project, or refusing to carry out assigned duties in order to do something that is more interesting, and never finishing the postponed work. Perpetrators of this pattern are the ones most disgusted by time and resource accounting systems and go to great lengths to sabotage them.

Category

- People

Related patterns

- Contrary to **activity imitation**, this behaviour is explicitly not related to the task at hand, making it easier to explain why said task is not progressing as a result.

IT Mismanagement Patterns

- **Global zero** is a related pattern insofar as important work doesn't get done; however, global zeros fail to deliver in a completely different fashion.

Doomed to success

A mode of operation without a place for failure. Situations that would normally count as definite signs of failure are ignored, information about them is withheld from stakeholders, and investment continues with a vague hope of success. Eventually, the whole affair is swept under the carpet in one way or another, the failure is never declared, and lessons are not learned from it.

Activities that are doomed to success can occasionally succeed, but ignoring the signs of problems makes it a lot harder. An undertaking of any significant complexity managed this way would have a very low chance of a real (as opposed to declared) success.

Category

- Fact-based environment

IT Mismanagement Patterns

Related patterns

- Activities that are doomed to success often become **cost sinks** and **death marches**.

- **Troglodyte managers** are particularly susceptible to this pattern, as isolation prevents them from seeing the early signs of doom (or any signs of doom for that matter).

- If everyone is convinced that a project is sure to succeed, **protecting its business case** becomes much easier.

Patterns

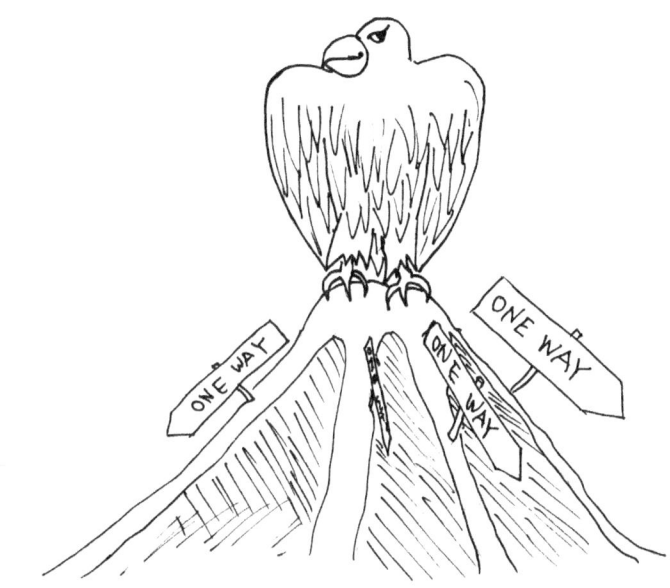

Einbahnstrasse[17]

Lack of feedback in the chain of command. More specifically, Einbahnstrasse is an arrangement where decisions are taken in one place, their effects are felt in another place, and the feedback mechanisms are dysfunctional or non-existent. This makes improvement based on feedback impossible and can lead to disastrous consequences if decision-makers mispredict the effect of their decisions.

Category

- Communication

---

[17]Einbahnstraße (German): One-way street.

IT Mismanagement Patterns

Related patterns

- **Management by hysteria** invariably builds Einbahnstrassen in order to avoid being distracted by logical arguments.

- **Pushers** are frequently there to prevent wrong-way driving.

- The **architectural answering machine** is an example of an Einbahnstrasse in architecture-related decision-making.

- Einbahnstrasse may form without express desire from management, for example, due to the historical **silence of the maltreated minds** or **global zeros** involved in the project.

- Planning failures such as **critical dependencies on imaginary assets** are much more likely when communication links are broken.

Patterns

Enterprise technology

Making technological choices based on promotional materials and buzzword compliance instead of analysing user requirements and features of the software; also believing that using big name products can remove the inherent complexity of the problem and automatically take care of non-functional aspects such as security and scalability. This usually results in selecting overhyped, expensive products from big vendors that have impressive lists of features that are irrelevant for the target application scenario.

Category

- Decision-making
- Business justification

IT Mismanagement Patterns

Related patterns

- Enterprise technologies are effective means of **Potemkin standard compliance**.

- The introduction of new enterprise technologies is often seen as important enough to become a **holy cow project**.

- Advocates of enterprise technology often use **lock, stock and barrel** reasoning for making technological choices or just go into **management by hysteria** mode. Any remaining dissonance between the platform of choice and the actual needs can be taken care of with **reverse requirements gathering**.

- **Responsibility outsourcing** is frequently the actual, if unpublished, driver for enterprise-laden choices. For some decision-makers, avoidance of responsibility happens to be so high on the agenda that preference for "enterprise" choices get enshrined in the **primal principles** of the said enterprise.

Patterns

Escalation of commitment

Continuing adherence to a suboptimal decision because acknowledging the mistake would be bad for the reputation. Escalation of commitment is often repeated several times, with the mistake being progressively harder to rectify and thus more difficult to acknowledge. This behaviour is similar to sunk cost fallacy and to **cost sink** pattern.

Category

- Fact-based environment
- Business justification

Related patterns

- **Disposable leaders** are frequently used as a circuit breaker for ongoing escalation of commitment.

IT Mismanagement Patterns

- In many cases, it might be possible to **fabricate a business case** for a suboptimal course of action. This mitigates the reputational damage thus ending the escalation of commitment or making it less severe.

Patterns

Every change is sacred[18]

The belief that every organisational change is good regardless of the nature of the change. Proponents of this way of thinking tend to perform a superficial or one-sided impact and business case analysis and focus on the implementation and marketing of the change to employees.

Category

- Fact-based environment
- Decision-making

Related patterns

- **Business case fabrication** is commonly used to rationalise changes that do not have a rationale otherwise.
- **Management by hysteria** is an application of this pattern to IT strategy.

---

[18]This refers to the "Every Sperm is Sacred" song from Monty Python's *The Meaning of Life*.

- This pattern is frequently invoked when justifying **suboptimal improvements**.

Patterns

Face transition

The switch from a "why don't we fix this?" attitude to "this is too difficult to fix now" or (sometimes) "this does not need to be fixed" that new employees undergo as they get more involved in sub-optimal decision-making and start feeling ownership of **common malpractices**.

Be attentive to what new hires say and empower them (and make them accountable) to deliver the changes they consider important.

Category

- People

Other related patterns

- Face transition is more likely in an organisation where being a **global zero** is the winning strategy.

- Face transition can be seen as a **scope drain** of the ambitions for positive change that the new employee might have had.

IT Mismanagement Patterns

Fake training

Training provided to staff solely as a means to disable the Luddites' typical defence that training in the new technology has not been provided. This is typically done by the cheapest bidder and at an inappropriate time, which means the marginal knowledge received in training cannot be applied in practice, and therefore quickly depreciates to the point when the only asset left with the trainee is the attendance certificate. Fake training is also provided to technical personnel so they can google solutions for the technology in question with the confidence of having the attendance certificate in their drawer. Finally, such training is provided to boost staff development statistics and formal indicators of availability of skills, so it can also be seen as a form of **activity imitation**.

Category

- People
- Business justification

Other related patterns

- Organisations that unconditionally support training of any kind make it a perfect way to **do other things**, which makes such training particularly attractive to **global zeros**.

- Lack of training is frequently quoted as the reason for slow adoption of new strategies and technologies. Fake training is, therefore, a frequent companion of **management by hysteria** and **wunderwaffe projects**.

- In organisations with **publicity-based valuation** cultures, training provided to end users may be employed to attract additional publicity, and therefore funding, to the project.

IT Mismanagement Patterns

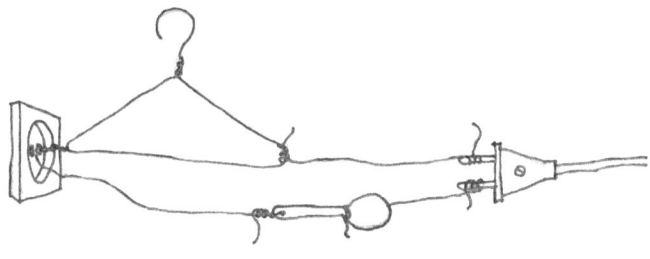

Faking ends meet

The practice of using any available financial resources to fund the most urgent need of the moment. In particular, faking ends meet involves funding unsustainable fixed costs with a lineup of cannibalised project budgets. This is widely used in **management by hysteria** and **escalation of commitment** to hide true costs from the sponsors, and may be an application of **Robin Hood financial management**.

Category

- Fact-based environment

Other related patterns

- Faking ends meet for managers is akin to **doing other things** for individual staff members.
- Faking ends meet is **submission to urgency** applied to the budget rather than time constraint.

Global zero

*The opposite of a **local hero**: an employee who is following all the procedures and rules but doesn't feel ownership of the end result. Formally everything is perfect, but the result is not achieved.* Performance management of global zeros is an obvious start, and it might provide a lead to deeper systemic problems in the organisation.

Category

- Recruitment
- People

Related patterns

- The majority of people are motivated by the final product or result of their work. Situations where meaningful results are unattainable for any single individual, such as in **runaway interdependence**, are breeding ground for global zeros.

IT Mismanagement Patterns

- Global zeros often appear in the organisation as **apples from the tree**. Given other alternatives, this should probably be considered a favourable outcome.

- For any **shadow governance**, it is of crucial importance to identify occasionally competent new hires and steer their **face transition** in a way that they end up in the **silence of the maltreated minds** rather than become global zeros.

- The **troglodyte manager** pattern describes an effective technique for being a global zero in a managerial position.

God mode[19]

A situation where decision-makers are isolated from the negative effects of their decisions and, as a result, are more willing to take unjustified risks. God mode conditions can form spontaneously, for example, due to an operating **Einbahnstrasse** or **guardian angels** at work.

Category

- Communication
- Decision-making

Other related patterns

- **Confirmation-biased reporting** and **silence of the maltreated minds** support switching of higher management levels into god mode.

- With all due respect and gratitude to the **local heroes** who keep many organisations afloat, they come with the disadvantage of frequently operating in god mode.

---

[19] God mode in some computer games is a feature/hack that prevents the character from being harmed and/or dying.

IT Mismanagement Patterns

- Managers operating in god mode are more likely to **fake ends meet** or do **Robin Hood financial management** as they only see the benefits of those practices and the information about harmful side-effects never reaches them.

Patterns

Goodbye party

Making important decisions or implementing significant changes shortly before leaving the organisation or retiring, so that most performance management and accountability mechanisms are no longer in effect.

The most disastrous goodbye parties are thrown by high-ranking managers just before retirement; they are typically referred to as "legacy" projects or other pretentious words to this effect.

Category

- Clear roles and responsibilities
- Planning

IT Mismanagement Patterns

Related patterns

- Good managers get themselves excused from making hiring decisions[20] long before they retire. Bad managers give their organisation some **apples from the tree** at their goodbye party.

- **Depreciation of commitment** might take care of some of the effects of a goodbye party. Unfortunately, it can't fix the responsibility vacuum arising from it.

- Declaring an **umph** in everything that one has ever started and never finished is very good for their pride and ambition and therefore extremely common as a goodbye party entertainment. Other related party games are **cutting the wrong corners** and **Robin Hood financial management**.

- Goodbye parties create ideal conditions for switching into **god mode** and having even more fun.

---

[20] It may be a formal responsibility that one cannot be excused from. What is meant here is substantive part of making this decision, not the actual signing at the dotted line.

Guardian angels

Rank and file employees who are sufficiently concerned with the good of the employer that they covertly sabotage particularly harmful management decisions. With their bad decisions secretly ignored and the good ones implemented forming a net-positive overall effect, managers lose reality checks as to the actual quality of their decision-making, and become overconfident about their abilities. Managers who excel in and profess their badness rely on guardian angels and the **McClane effect** to save the day when their constant walking on thin ice goes bad.

Category

- People
- Communication

IT Mismanagement Patterns

Related patterns

- **Local heroes** are sometimes motivated by their own understanding of an employer's good and therefore become guardian angels or even form mighty teams of guardian angels that may take the function of **shadow governance**.

- Similarly to **silence of the maltreated minds**, guardian angels suppress feedback to managerial decisions. This reinforces the **Einbahnstrasse** that isolates management from the results of their actions and leads them to the perils of **god mode**.

- **Pushers** are the nemeses of guardian angels: they get their paycheck specifically to mitigate the guardian angels "problem".

Guilt-based management

Fabricating a sense of guilt in subordinates to make them more prone to manipulation. An employee feeling guilty and seeking redemption can then be easily coerced to work long hours, accept excessive personal responsibility or cooperate in morally questionable practices.

Category

- People
- Clear roles and responsibilities

Related patterns

- **Beam in the eye fallacy** is instrumental in planting guilt.

IT Mismanagement Patterns

- Guilt emerges by itself in collectives that have to deliver to **deadline-driven estimates** or are manning **death marches**.

- **Doing other things** and **global zeros** are sometimes intentionally tolerated by management to manufacture guilt.

Highlander[21] principle

Declaring one software vendor or platform the solution for all IT needs of the organisation and believing that this is the most efficient way of running IT.

The Highlander principle is usually implemented as a means of promoting someone's political agenda rather than a thought-out platform selection strategy. Constraining all IT activities to products from one company is not a viable option, except in trivial cases, as no single vendor can provide all the necessary software. In the real world, the Highlander principle requires a system of exceptions, which often turns out to be rather arbitrary.

---

[21] Refers to a story of the centuries-old war between immortal warriors that can possibly stop only when there are no more enemies to face for the last one, depicted in the namesake cult movie. The tagline of the movie goes "there can be only one".

IT Mismanagement Patterns

Category

- Decision-making
- Fact-based environment

Related patterns

- The **architectural answering machine** is a possible implementation of the Highlander Principle.

- This principle comes in handy for instituting **management by hysteria** and justifying **holy cow** and **wunderwaffe projects**.

Patterns

Holy cow project

A project that is perceived to be so important that normal rules regarding business justification do not apply.

When working on a holy cow project, project proponents typically get away with presenting completely bogus business cases (or none at all) to their management. Holy cow projects usually result from **circular decision**-making with the subsequent **escalation of commitment** and involve **write-only documents**.

Category

- Business justification

Other related patterns

- Holy cow projects are a canonical case of **business case fabrication**. The latter is a broader pattern, as business justification happens to be fabricated in less important projects as well.

- In the absence of express business justification, holy cow projects only occasionally happen to create value, so most of them are destined to become **cost sinks** and end in an **umph**.

- When success criteria are vaguely defined at best and failure is not an option the project is sure to be **doomed to success**.

Holy rodeo

*Inflating the scope of a **holy cow project**. Holy cow projects have a fiat business case that won't be affected by changing their scope, so new functionality automatically gains a business case (so it "rides the holy cow").* Amateurs will counterbalance their rodeo with a **scope drain** to avoid creating an impression that their project has become too big. Professionals know that the holy cow is **doomed to success** and will ride it fearlessly.

Category

- Business justification

IT Mismanagement Patterns

Hope[22] based estimation

Estimating the time and resources needed to implement a project without having a plan or detailed understanding of the work involved. In many cases of hope based estimation, the person producing the estimate has never done a similar project.

Category

- Planning
- Fact-based environment

Other related patterns

- **Deadline-driven estimation** is a related technique. The

---

[22]It can be argued that any estimate comes with an inherent risk (see Prov. 19:21 for details). Here, we define "hope" as unmanaged risk.

two are a natural match since vacuous estimates can be resized to fit the deadline without any loss of precision.

- Hope based estimates are commonly used in **write-only documents** that are believed to contain business justification. Still, such estimates alone do not constitute **business case fabrication** as they make baseless claims rather than fraudulent ones.

- **Local heroes**, who happen to mistake their proven competence to execute for competence to do anything, are frequently off by miles in their estimates because of their hopes and false self-confidence

- Mild cases of **faking ends meet** may happen due to the hopes that in the end there will be enough money for everything.

IT Mismanagement Patterns

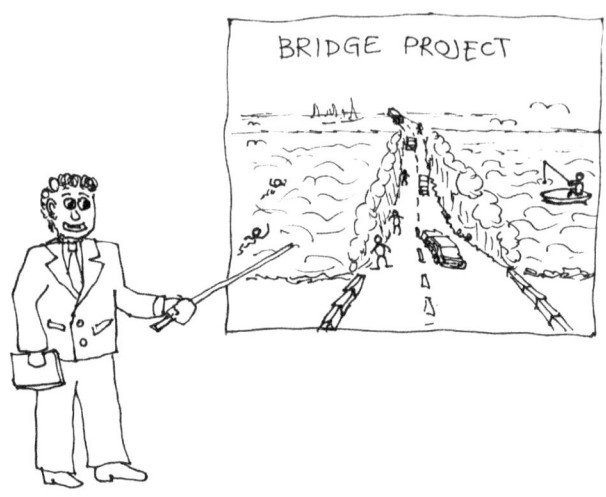

Imaginary superpower

A form of **critical dependency on imaginary assets** where a plan is based on bluff authority assertions and/or assumption of ability to change the elements, such as the way Internet works, solely by administrative means of the organisation or an individual manager.

Category

- Fact-based environment

Other related patterns

- Managers guilty of the **assertion of culture** are likely to overestimate their ability to drive change in other areas as well.

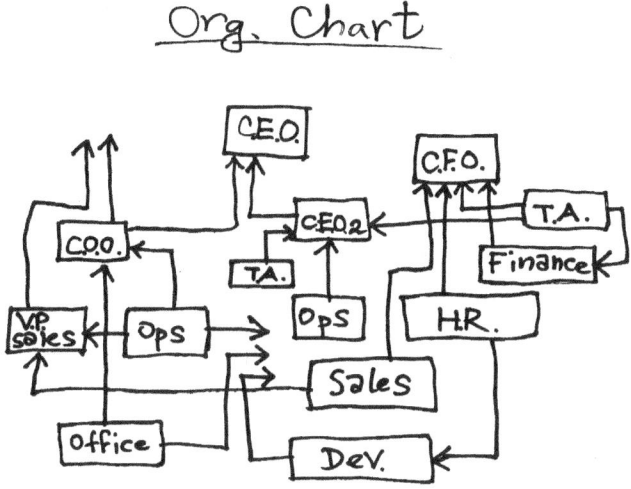

Irrational unified process (a.k.a. Avalanche model)

Attempt to combine waterfall[23] model with an iterative approach or to use agile[24] practices by a manager who has poor understanding of agile methodology (and often of software development in general). The result is a sorry concoction of disadvantages of both approaches where low flexibility and late delivery are combined with poorly documented requirements, fragmented design and unclear process.

Category

- Planning
- Clear roles and responsibilities

---

[23] https://en.wikipedia.org/wiki/Waterfall_model
[24] https://en.wikipedia.org/wiki/Agile_software_development

IT Mismanagement Patterns

Related patterns

- As development methods are susceptible to the variability of fashion, they constitute an additional playing field for **management by hysteria**.

- Users of the pattern tend to turn a blind eye to the failings of the approach and instead blame developers (or software development in general), joining the ranks of those fearing the **risk of programming**.

- Responsibility and ownership of concerns are often the first to be muddled by unclear processes. This enables flexible blame delegation and creates fertile ground for **guilt-based management**.

Patterns

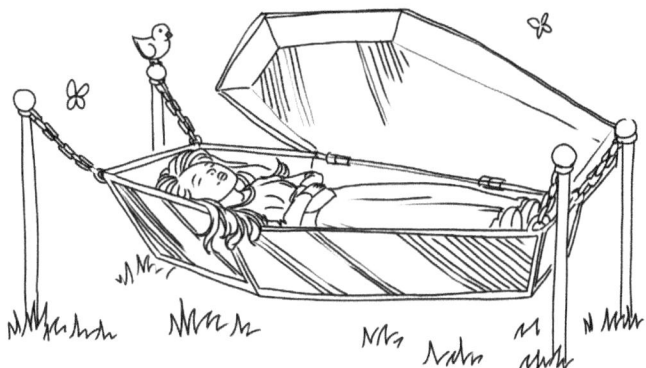

Late awakening

Strategic stubbornness in the face of evidence that the plan is not realistic until the last moment. As the deadlines draw nearer and the probability of delivery while following the preferred strategy tends toward zero, the management might become more open to using any means available to save the situation and deliver at least something. This leads to unneeded stress, waste of resources and suboptimal results as compared to what would be possible if the problems were recognised and addressed earlier.

Category

- Planning

Related patterns

- **Cutting the wrong corners** might turn just about workable plan into an utterly impossible one. Acknowledging this

IT Mismanagement Patterns

fact will inevitably come late since success was still in principle possible earlier.

- Late awakening is the death agony of a **management by hysteria** cycle and the pain incurred therein might easily motivate the next hysteria.

- **Scope drain** may be used to avoid late awakening or to mitigate its adverse effects. In particularly hopeless cases the former will only delay the inevitable.

- Late awakening is the phase when **McClane effect** is most visible. It is not uncommon for management not only to recall that they have competent employees, but also to come up with disingenuous ways of making them accountable for delivering the product under impossible time and resource constraints (as in **cast iron triangle**), or even culpable for the strategy's prior struggles (as in **guilt-based management**).

- **Business case protectionism** can make the late awakening even later and more severe.

Patterns

Local hero

A person known to be able to solve IT problems and produce results, who is contacted by the customers directly, bypassing official communication channels.

A local hero is often at least partially content with the situation, feeling indispensable and motivated. Such arrangements reduce transparency and can lead to problems later because normal procedures and frameworks are bypassed. However, in the organisations that are rendered dysfunctional by **runaway interdependence** and other systemic issues, local heroism might be the only way to get anything done for the people who don't have the power to fix the system. The only other alternative is becoming a **global zero**[25].

---

[25] "It's better to be a local hero than a global zero" — a nameless Local Hero

IT Mismanagement Patterns

Category

- People
- Recruitment
- Clear roles and responsibilities

Related patterns

- Local heroes, overworked with getting stuff done and skipping steps that are not essential, are frequently attacked by the proud bearers of a **beam in the eye** with accusations of **cutting the wrong corners**, introducing the **risk of programming** and other formal violations.

- If management does not improve for a long time, local heroes might self-organise into **shadow governance** structures. This process can also be triggered by centralisation of IT gone astray, in which local heroes find themselves in the same boat with others whom they see as possible collaborators, all of them feeling unhappy with the direction where things are going.

- Local heroes rarely say "no" and often don't have time and patience for proper planning, which leads to essentially **hope based** and **deadline-driven estimation** if any estimates are produced at all.

- Local heroes tend to practice **Highlander principle**, with their one true platform being the platform they know best.

Patterns

Lock, stock and barrel

An architectural approach that is based on the assumption that an "80% solution" to every problem may be delivered by combining features of commercial off-the-shelf (COTS) software without significant effort or custom development.

This might seem attractive in terms of up-front cost, but some critical requirements often end up in the unfulfilled 20%. Unfulfilled critical requirements[26] lead to degradation of performance of affected business processes through inevitable **manualisation**.

---

[26] "Unfulfilled critical requirements" is an oxymoron. If they are indeed critical, you don't have a solution. If they are not, why call them critical? Options that do not meet all critical requirements should be discarded. Then you can pick the one that makes the loudest bang for the buck. All the 80/20 business is only good for confusing oneself and others.

IT Mismanagement Patterns

Category

- Decision-making
- Quality

Related patterns

- **Risk of programming** is often named as a reason for such approach.

- **Architectural answering machines**, obsessed with control and reduction of technologies used, and oblivious of actual business needs tend to recommend lock, stock and barrel solutions.

- An important difference from **buy before you think** is that thinking is happening but the assumptions about requirements and the expected product quality are wrong.

- Lock, stock and barrel approach creates ideal conditions for **confirmation-biased reporting**: being vaguely fit for purpose, the solution delivers to some of the requirements from the initial scope which can be used as evidence that it meets all of the requirements.

- Apart from not delivering to critical requirements, the lock, stock and barrel solutions deliver to non-critical requirements and non-requirements, creating fertile ground for **reverse requirements gathering**.

Lock-in discount

Underestimating the cost of a project when proposing it to the customer and inflating the cost later when the customer is no longer in the position to choose an alternative approach. A lock-in discount can be intentional or accidental. In the former case the service provider is aware that the cost will be greater but fears that if it's honestly reported, the project will not be accepted. The latter case is a genuine failure of cost estimation. Lock-in discount can be repeated multiple times when the cost estimate is raised in steps to make it impossible to demonstrate that the business case is no longer viable (this usually turns the project into a **cost sink**).

Category

- Planning
- Fact-based environment

IT Mismanagement Patterns

Other related patterns

- It is common for **buy before you think** environments to use the low cost of an off-the-shelf product that as an argument in favour of buying it. That the product does not solve the problem it is supposed to solve is only realised later, when it is too late to back out because the project is already **doomed to success**.

- **Scope drain** is an effective tool for the management of the project once it has cashed in on the lock-in discount.

- Lock-in discount can be seen as a form of **unbribe**[27].

---

[27] Lock-in discount differs from more typical cases of unbribery by more active involvement of the unbriber, but it still fits the definition.

Looking into the future

The refutation of practical arguments based on historical evidence by asserting that in the future the situation will be different, so the arguments don't apply.

In most cases, no roadmap or other assurance of change is provided by the one promoting looking into the future; simply stating that future will be different is deemed to be a valid counterargument. The most skilled lookouts use this pattern in discussions about decisions with life expectancies so short the alleged future is guaranteed not to come before the decision loses relevance.

Category

- Fact-based environment.

IT Mismanagement Patterns

Related patterns

- Looking into the future enables the perpetrators to introduce **critical dependencies on imaginary assets**: there are practical difficulties with stating that something exists now when it doesn't; whether it will exist in the future is inherently probabilistic[28] and can, therefore, be argued either way.

- Looking into the future when arranging a **goodbye party** can increase its impact and is absolutely safe. Nobody can tell you "I told you" when you're no longer around.

---

[28]See https://en.wikipedia.org/wiki/Interpretations_of_quantum_mechanics for further debate on this issue.

Patterns

Management by hysteria

A style of strategic IT management where the organisation goes through the phases of excessive belief in the capabilities of certain software platform or methodology (hysterias).

During a hysteria, the platform of choice (POC) is considered to be the solution to all IT needs and the strategy emphasises migration of all IT activities to that particular platform. Hysterias are usually followed by remissions when the limitations of the POC and complexities of migration projects are appreciated. After the capabilities and limitations of a POC are better understood, the strong sides of it could be exploited to finally reap some benefits. Alternatively, perhaps it's time for another hysteria!

Category

- Decision-making
- Business justification.

IT Mismanagement Patterns

Related patterns

- The **Highlander principle** describes one cycle of management by hysteria.

- Management by hysteria dramatically inflates the amount of change and churn that IT environment has to undergo. It can, therefore, be used as a very efficient form of **activity imitation**.

- Having usually little to show in the way of actual business justification, hysterias require decision-making support in the form of **business case fabrication**, **business case protectionism**, **reverse requirements gathering** and **every change is sacred** mentality.

- Conversations with managers exhibiting high-level convictions not supported by technical understanding or detailed strategy tend to frustrate engineers and lead to the **silence of the maltreated minds**.

- Unable to measure and understand the actual business impact of its activities, management hysterias tend to produce **suboptimal improvements** and celebrate them as progress.

- Hysterias often emerge from expensive consultancies procured for **strategy outsourcing**.

Manager in absentia

A manager who strongly asserts their authority while not being in the office enough to either keep up-to-date with changing business contexts or even take necessary day-to-day decisions.

Taking a decision for a manager in absentia leads to scandal and sabotage of its execution later on. Responsibility for delays in projects caused by the dependency on manager in absentia ends up with project managers.

Category

- People
- Clear roles and responsibilities

IT Mismanagement Patterns

Related patterns

- In many cases, **troglodyte managers** eventually realise that becoming a manager in absentia tremendously improves one's peace of mind.

- Being physically removed from the assigned post offers help and protection in **doing other things**.

- Management absenteeism can be the key factor in the growth of informal authority of **shadow governance**: it might be shadow, but at least it's there!

Patterns

Manager-in-the-middle attack

Adding management layers that hinder communication between customers and service providers.

Sometimes inserted managers have their own agenda or priorities, sometimes they just add overheads without adding value. In particularly bad cases the relationship can completely break down.

Category

- Clear roles and responsibilities
- People

Related patterns

- A manager-in-the-middle might be a **disposable leader**, and the attack might represent an attempt to stealthily eliminate the service.

- Chains of indirection between the customer and the service provider are fertile soil for **news improvement** and **confirmation-biased reporting**.

IT Mismanagement Patterns

- Managers in the middle, ignorant about either the customer needs or the technical constraints of the project, are also more susceptible to commit grave estimation sins, such as **hope based estimation** and **deadline-driven estimation**.

- Manager-in-the-middle attacks can be circumvented by **local heroes**, **guardian angels** and **shadow governance**.

Patterns

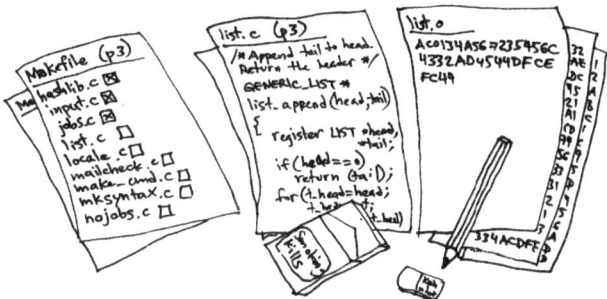

Manualisation

A change in the business process or automation software that transforms previously automatic operation into manual work. Manualisation may be justified, for example, if the volume of the operations is small and the desired flexibility is hard to achieve via existing automated process. More often though it's a step back that results from the implementation of **suboptimal improvements**.

Category

- Business justification

Other related patterns

- Manualisation of highly repetitive processes is a good way to achieve operational **activity imitation**

IT Mismanagement Patterns

McClane effect[29]

*The tendency to ignore specialist advice and make decisions based on high-level considerations (such as **responsibility delegation**, the **primacy of principles**, **management by hysteria**, etc.) unless there's a crisis.* When problems come, technically competent employees are summoned to save the day but then again ignored when steering the strategy.

Category

- Decision-making
- People

---

[29]This refers to New York policeman John McClane, the protagonist of the *Die Hard* [12] series, portrayed in the film by Bruce Willis. The character has issues with conduct and respect to authority, which are giving him a lot of grief at work and at home. However, he is extremely efficient at what he does, which allows him to single-handedly handle crises time and time again.

Other related patterns

- Unless availability of the above-mentioned technically competent employees is closely monitored, which is rarely the case, it may well happen that said employees have pursued greener pastures by the time their help is sought. Carelessness in retention of these resources of last resort is a form of **critical dependency on imaginary assets**.

- The McClane effect is, essentially, a sign of management's awareness, but not recognition, of **shadow governance** and the network of **local heroes** in the organisation.

IT Mismanagement Patterns

News improvement

Deliberately misleading stakeholders about delivery status and withholding information about problems in the course of a project to ensure continuous buy-in and funding.

The source of the improved news often becomes subject to the **escalation of commitment** as further, sometimes greater, news improvement becomes necessary to ensure that the illusion of progress is maintained.

Category

- Fact-based environment

Other related patterns

- **Confirmation-biased reporting** is a form of news improvement that is more robust in terms of plausible deniability.

- **Hope based estimation** and **deadline-driven estimation** may create an enormous amount of goodwill from sponsors at the beginning of the project, while **quantity assurance** and **doomed to success** *modus operandi* are good for maintaining this goodwill until the bitter end.

- News about a project that is actively **cutting the wrong corners**, while technically true, should also be considered improved.

- Names of **local heroes** who don't have any influence on the subject matter may be included in communications as mascots of trust.

- A **lock-in discount** is an example of news improvement in sales.

IT Mismanagement Patterns

Pareto[30] denial

The rejection of opportunities to deliver value or improve efficiency where it would not require additional resources, increase risk or reduce the quality of any other part of an organisation's activities.

The reasons for Pareto denial are typically bogus and refer to the interests of **holy cow projects**, **wunderwaffe projects**, the **primacy of principles** or other untouchable activities and beliefs.

Category

- Business justification

---

[30]This refers to Pareto efficiency — an ideal state of an economic system where it is impossible to improve the well-being of any one of the participants without damaging the well-being of at least one of the others. Any improvements that don't damage someone else's well-being are considered worth making.

Other related patterns

- Pareto denial is an important device of **business case protectionism**.

- Once Pareto denial has been mastered, a decision-maker may proceed to mandating **suboptimal improvements**, **manualisation** or getting rid of **tainted knowledge** on their way to perfecting IT mismanagement.

- In an environment with **publicity-based valuation**, good opportunities may be rejected because they are unlikely to become visible to the top management.

IT Mismanagement Patterns

Potemkin[31] standard compliance

Formal adherence to the standard to emanate maturity. This differs from **cargo cult standard compliance** in that only the *appearance* of maturity is important here.

Category

- Fact-based environment

Related patterns

- **Write-only documents** are the chief tool of Potemkin standard compliance. They are cheap to create, and individuals who are willing to produce them are receptive to being

---

[31] This comes from "Potemkin villages" — state-of-the-art villages built by Russian minister Grigory Potemkin along the way of travel of Empress Catherine II the Great, to whom he was secretly married, to impress her with Russia's riches under his rule and conceal the actual grim picture.

handed acceptance criteria such as the number of pages, images or ISO standard references, etc., in the final document.

- Potemkin standard compliance can be seen as deliberate **activity imitation** applied to standard compliance.

IT Mismanagement Patterns

Primacy of principles[32]

A blanket declaration of a set of abstract principles as the top level reference point for all decision-making.

There is subsequent indiscriminate use of said principles without any consideration of their applicability to a particular situation. This can easily lead to suboptimal choices, short-sighted decisions and non-implementable designs. Even more importantly, faith in any unquestionable absolute is fundamentally incompatible with a fact-based environment.

Category

- Decision-making
- Fact-based environment

---

[32]The name is borrowed from an example in TOGAF. It is unlikely that TOGAF's authors intended this example to elicit consequences described in the namesake mismanagement pattern, but its formulation is music to the ears of any manager with control issues for whose convenience we offer the pattern in this book.

Related patterns

- Adoption of the primacy of principles significantly simplifies the operation of **architectural answering machines** and provides solid justification for **common malpractice**, **split personality order** and for proposals to **turn into hedgehogs**.

- The primacy of principles often leads to **beam in the eye fallacy** as healthy projects that are not aligned with the principles are seen as more broken than the dysfunctional ones that follow them.

IT Mismanagement Patterns

Publicity-based valuation

The practice of assigning value and, consequently, funding to projects on the basis of their visibility to upper management. This is typically manifested by organisations that overfund trivially scoped user-facing "eye candy" and underfund infrastructure that delivers actual new capabilities.

Category

- Business justification

Related patterns

- Managers often turn to this pattern when they are looking for a method to maximise the efficiency of their **activity imitation**.

- The practice can also be applied inside a project where similar results may be achieved by **cutting the wrong corners**.

- One way to get the attention of top management is to spend big. Using **enterprise technology** is, therefore, a great way to increase the perceived value of your project. Another way is to talk about industry standards and compliance. Here, **Potemkin standard compliance** comes in handy.

IT Mismanagement Patterns

Pusher (a.k.a. Loyal facade)

A middle manager who is appointed to force subordinates to do something that they are refusing to do.

This pattern is used by managers who can't convince their staff with arguments or otherwise, so they hire a pusher to make it their problem.

Category

- People
- Clear roles and responsibilities

Related patterns

- Pushers are often used as barrier troops for facilitating **death marches**.

- While pushers are meant to be bad news only for staff executing the project, their involvement inevitably turns into a **manager-in-the-middle attack** with negative consequences for the clients and the project in general.

IT Mismanagement Patterns

```
def test_send_request():
    # env = make_env()              #FIXME: fails randomly
    # response = env.send_request(URL)   #FIX: need env
    assert True  # response.code == OK
    assert 1     # response.value == EXPECTED
    #env.clean_up()   #TODO: uncomment when have env
```

Quantity assurance

The testing and attestation of quality of a product by unqualified or perversely interested individuals for the sake of clocking a plausible quantity of effort hours for the mandatory "testing" deliverable found in any project plan. Quantity assurance is typically allowed to happen either by decision-makers whose accountability is time-limited (**responsibility outsourcing** vendors) or by executives carried away by **submission to urgency**. It can be prevented by defining a project quality plan at the beginning of the project.

Category

- Quality

Other related patterns

- Quantity assurance may also be performed for the purposes of **Potemkin standard compliance**.
- The inherent infallibility of **holy cow projects** creates a disincentive to test their products well.

Quick fix of doom

A hastily implemented temporary solution that stays in operation much longer than originally intended.

A quick fix of doom is fast-tracked to cover the absolute necessities with the intention to replace it with a permanent solution as soon as possible. Any normal considerations that would be in place for implementing the change are forgone because of the urgency and the temporary nature of the arrangement. By relieving the acute pressure to solve the problem, the quick fix of doom often means the proper implementation is postponed indefinitely.

Category

- Quality
- Planning

IT Mismanagement Patterns

Related patterns

- To the unenlightened, the quick fix of doom appears to have solved the problem. This can lead to **critical dependency on imaginary assets**.

- In projects planned using a **deadline-driven estimation** technique, it is not unusual to observe the entire scope delivered as a patchwork of quick fixes of doom.

- It is much quicker and easier to write when you are not asked to make your writing readable. **Write-only documents** are therefore very popular as quick fixes of doom for documentation needs.

- Quick fixes of doom are often used to solve a Zeitnot created by **late awakening**, thus making the damage permanent.

Responsibility delegation

A manager making a decision in the competence area of their subordinates and forcing it down on them for execution. The people tasked with the implementation become responsible for the consequences of a decision they didn't take and couldn't influence, while the manager evades responsibility they ought to be carrying with pride. If the decision turns out to be a bad one, the technique provides the manager with the short-term benefit of averting blame. Should the decision, accidentally, turn out to be a good one, the fact the manager was behind it enables them to demonstrate how everything is right with management and wrong with the staff.

With sufficient mastery in ambiguity on the part of the manager, it may become impossible to tell whether the responsibility for the decision lay with them or with staff until it is clear whether this decision was a good one. Skilled delegators, therefore, emanate responsibility in a quantum superposition of being delegated and retained, and the blame-function collapse happens after the results are in.

IT Mismanagement Patterns

Category

- Clear roles and responsibilities

Related patterns

- When scope, time and budget are agreed, and buy-in from the team is registered, i.e. the team is responsible for delivering, it is typical for managers to start **cutting the wrong corners** to create the image of strong and early success. Inevitable problems caused by the havoc in scheduling are addressed by the manager using **guilt-based management** techniques.

- Responsibility can also be delegated laterally — in **circular decisions** or to a **disposable leader**, or even upwards through **responsibility escalation** or in case a **goodbye party** is looming.

- Standardising an **avalanche model** for project management is a clever and highly popular way to delegate responsibility.

Patterns

Responsibility escalation

*A clever form of **circular decision**: giving advice to high-level decision-makers on technical matters, and after the decision is taken based on this advice, referring to it as justification for the chosen course of action.*

Another form of responsibility escalation is withholding valid but undesirable options from the decision-makers, and after the choice has been made based on incomplete information, using it as an argument against the options that have never been presented to decision-makers.

Category

- Documentation and reporting
- Fact-based environment

IT Mismanagement Patterns

Other related patterns

- This pattern is an example of how **apple from the tree** recruitment practices can backfire. Incompetence and dishonesty are general-purpose weapons: one day they may be aimed at the one who introduced them into the organisation.

- Responsibility escalation is a powerful tool for **business case fabrication** in environments where fiat business justifications are a norm or where executive decisions are implemented in a manner indistinguishable from the one used to implement regulatory requirements.

Responsibility outsourcing

Hiring an external entity to take responsibility for decisions, actions or inaction of staff members.

Common examples of responsibility outsourcing are **strategy laundering** or **virtual support contract**. If anything goes wrong, the external entity is blamed, typically when its engagement and any possibility of recourse have long expired.

Category

- Clear roles and responsibilities

Related patterns

- The highly common practice of engaging a consultant to analyse the situation with regard to some enterprise area

IT Mismanagement Patterns

of concern[33] and to recommend a solution is, essentially, **business case fabrication** with outsourced responsibility.

- In case of **strategy outsourcing** the responsibility is also outsourced but that is the least of the problems.

---

[33]The authors have long debated whether "enterprise area of concern" should be made into a pattern of its own. What it refers to is one of the definitely important but excruciatingly boring areas, like accounting, record management or compliance. Those rarely attract interest from rockstars on board and therefore end up with staff who are less competent and more hungry for confirmation of reasons for their existence.

Patterns

Reverse business justification

Declaring any deliverable of a project to be a benefit even if nobody ever wanted it or asked for it. Sometimes the deliverable is actually a disbenefit, for example, **manualisation** of some high volume activity, but arguments are found or made up to present the result in a positive light.

Category

- Business justification

Other related patterns

- **Business case fabrication** — a practice that takes more effort to achieve the same result — may be used by less experienced practitioners.

IT Mismanagement Patterns

- **Einbahnstrassen** greatly facilitate the application of this pattern because in the absence of working feedback mechanisms it becomes easier to declare anything a benefit.

- **Every change is sacred** is a trivial but surprisingly effective (and supported by literature) tactic for justifying just about anything.

- **Holy cow projects** are usually, at least in part, reverse-justified.

Patterns

Reverse requirements gathering

Developing requirements for a software solution based on the capabilities of the preconceived choice of platform instead of the needs of the stakeholders.

Often used to reinforce the business case of using a single platform for all needs as in the **Highlander principle** and **architectural answering machine**.

Category

- Fact-based environment
- Documentation and reporting

Related patterns

- This pattern allows a quick **umph** when dealing with the aftermath of **buy before you think** and other defective decision strategies.

IT Mismanagement Patterns

- Solutions in search of a problem that trigger this pattern are usually the product of **suboptimal improvements** or a **wunderwaffe** project.

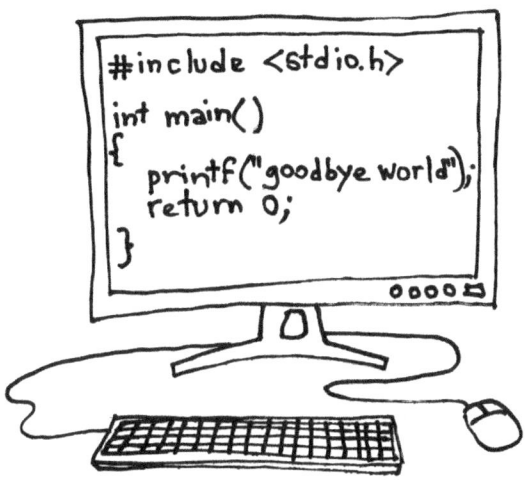

Risk of programming

The belief that bespoke code presents high business risk and therefore should be avoided at all costs.

Custom development is indeed rarely justified when complete out-of-the-box alternatives are available. However, as soon as the tailoring of the ready-made software exceeds simple configuration, programming becomes increasingly more attractive due to the higher process maturity, greater flexibility, and better maintainability that it allows.

Category

- Decision-making

IT Mismanagement Patterns

Related patterns

- When deciding in favour of custom development, the manager loses the ability to **outsource responsibility** to the vendor. Even when custom development is outsourced, requirements elicitation is usually the manager's accountability.

- Custom solutions usually have a humble appearance and minimal, if any, marketing materials. They are not certified for compliance with famous but irrelevant standards that nobody actually understands. All in all, they make poor material for **Potemkin standard compliance**.

- Past programming is certainly no less risky than future programming and should likewise be avoided. **Suboptimal improvements** (for example **manualisation**) can be implemented to replace existing solutions that are seen as too risky.

Robin Hood[34] financial management

Shifting resources from projects or services that deliver steadily and efficiently and therefore enjoy clients' willingness to pay, to projects that are failing or have already failed, to which clients are unwilling to provide any additional funding.

Category

- Business justification

Related patterns

- This pattern may be seen as analogous to **doing other things** but for decision-makers rather than rank and file staff.

---

[34]English folklore hero outlaw known for robbing from the rich and giving to the poor.

IT Mismanagement Patterns

- Managers are often coerced into taking from the rich and giving to the poor under the duress of **guilt-based management** exercised by the stakeholders of a failing project.

- Robin Hood financial management breaks project containment, which lets **cost sinks** and **death marches** affect a bigger part of the organisation and do more damage.

Runaway interdependence

The excessive specialisation and distribution of responsibilities between different units and employees in an organisation so that any project of even minimal complexity has to involve many people from different departments.

This leads to complicated interaction patterns and other overheads that are capable of killing the business case for any project up to a particular, large enough, scale. Runaway interdependence thus incapacitates the organisation to take on smaller projects, and de-motivates employees as they become too remote from the customers and seemingly incapable of delivering results on their own. One of the drivers of runaway interdependence is concentrating the power to get anything done in the hands of few people. In such situations, employees often have to bypass the rules in **local hero** fashion or follow them and become **global zeros**.

IT Mismanagement Patterns

Category

- People

Other related patterns

- If you cannot do anything small, everything starts looking big. Moreover, if the budget is not unlimited, you will normally be able to do fewer big things than you could, theoretically, do small ones. This predicament is a breeding ground for rationalising the **Highlander principle**.

- Interdependence may work if all of the expectations from all actors are easily enforceable by those who "need" the result. If this is not the case, introducing such interdependence becomes as dysfunctional as any **split personality order**.

- Runaway interdependence is an example of **common malpractice**, which is why it is stubbornly kept around by management.

- Being unable to do anything of value without bureaucracy and cooperation from people who do not care is soul-crushing and thus contributes to **face transition**.

- Although to the authors' knowledge there is no standard for a one-size-fits-all organisational structure, runaway interdependence is widely seen as a matter of **cargo cult standard compliance**.

- **Doing other things** is much easier when you're always blocked by dependencies, so no-one expects any tangible result from your work any time soon.

Patterns

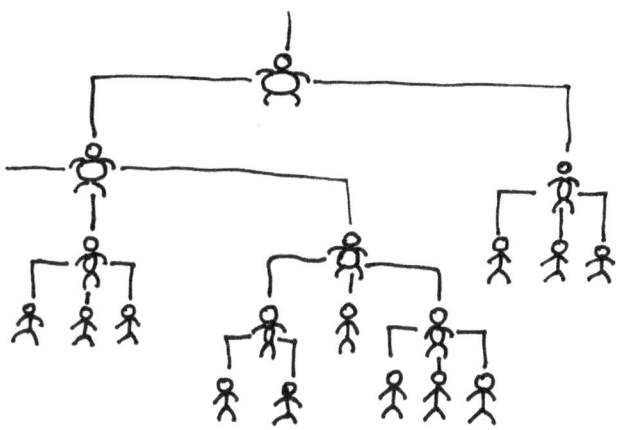

Scale of economies

Inflating the size of a department (or merging multiple departments) under the guise of creating economies of scale but with actual purpose of upgrading the managerial post that oversees the department and gaining decision-making power over a higher budget.

This leads to a higher total remuneration for the person occupying the said managerial post, increasing the scale of their household economy, hence the name.

Category

- Fact-based environment

Related patterns

- **Business case fabrication** and similar techniques can be used to create the justification for inflation of the department.

IT Mismanagement Patterns

- Various **concealed consensus**, **responsibility escalation** and **responsibility outsourcing** techniques can be used by the initiator of the change to protect themselves when it becomes clear that no benefit to the organisation was achieved.

- Maintaining and justifying the scale of economies is made easier by its own effects: **cutting the wrong corners** is easier to hide when delivery team is further away from the customer; **Robin Hood financial management** and **faking ends meet** are both more efficient and produce results of better longevity on a larger scale; finally, the **news can be improved** even further with a few more hand-offs.

Scope drain

Hollowing out the expected result of a project in order to decrease the impact of non-delivery. This can be achieved by implementing **quick fixes of doom** or finding other reasons to discard parts of the scope. It is commonly used, often together with the **depreciation of commitment**, to alleviate tensions created by the **escalation of commitment** or in **wunderwaffe projects**. Scope drain can be facilitated by ambiguity and broad interpretation of **write-only documents** planted into the project at an earlier date.

Category

- Planning
- Documentation and reporting

Other related patterns

- Scope drain is often called for when it becomes clear that the solution chosen using a **lock, stock and barrel** approach delivers the wrong 80% of functionality, essential requirements are not met, and there is no budget to fix this within the project.

Patterns

Shadow governance

Alternative information flow and control structures that evolve when formal communication channels and hierarchy are not working.

Shadow governance can be used to work around **troglodyte managers**, **runaway interdependence**, **Einbahnstrassen**, the **McClane effect** and **architectural answering machines**. Such arrangements, when they are called for, tactically improve the functioning of the organisation, but they decrease its manageability and transparency.

Category

- Clear roles and responsibilities
- People

IT Mismanagement Patterns

Other related patterns

- As an informal structure with no legal authority, shadow governance often has to employ techniques such as **circular decisions** and **concealed consensus** to obfuscate the origin of the decisions.

- A very positive side of shadow governance is its ability to debunk unfair, manipulative and deceptive practices employed by management. Shadow governance often gets the message straight in cases of **death marches**, **guilt-based management**, **responsibility delegation** and proposals to **turn into hedgehogs**.

Patterns

Silence of the maltreated minds

A lack of feedback on strategy direction and specific management decisions from the specialists, caused by losing hope of being seriously considered or heard at all.

The disappearance of feedback is often misinterpreted by management as consent or arrival at the acceptance stage of the change curve[35].

Category

- People

---

[35]The Kubler-Ross change curve is a model depicting personal attitudes towards change as going from shock and denial through anger and depression to eventual acceptance and integration.

Related patterns

- **Einbahnstrasse** arrangements can lead to the silence of the maltreated minds and be further reinforced by it.

- The **McClane effect** is a powerful demotivator for staff and one of the most common reasons for the fall of silence.

- **Troglodyte managers** ignore undesirable information to produce similar effects and sometimes manufacture silence of the maltreated minds on purpose.

- One of the winning tactics in an unsafe environment is to withhold information about your activities and opinions to avert blame. It is therefore common for the silence of the maltreated minds to quickly develop where **guilt-based management** is practised.

Patterns

Split personality order[36]

Structuring accountability and reporting in a manner that is incompatible with the organisation's administrative buildup.

The most common scenario is the imposition of a functional matrix on a strongly hierarchical organisation.

Category

- Clear roles and responsibilities

---

[36]Split personality disorder (currently formally called "dissociative identity disorder") is a rare mental disorder that manifests by multiple personalities occupying the same body. The personalities ("alters") may have different age, sex, nationalities, intellects and worldviews so they steer behavior in markedly different ways while each claiming sole control and discretion over the person's actions.

Related patterns

- **Assertion of culture** is a more general pattern, of which split personality order is one example.

- **God mode** conditions can be created when someone is given the power to decide certain things, but the related responsibility assignment is not enforceable.

- New accountability and lines of reporting may be a part of a fashionable management standard that is being forced on the organisation for **cargo cult standard compliance**. Little attention is given to the details of how the new structure will function, essentially commanding the people inhabiting this figment of the manager's imagination to **turn into hedgehogs**.

- Split personality order may be used as a way to make true command chains less obvious and conceal the true source of the decisions. This use case is similar to a **circular decision** and **concealed consensus**.

- **Shadow governance** is an alternative control structure that evolves by itself rather than being asserted like in this pattern.

Patterns

Strategy laundering

Hiring an external entity to perform analysis and recommend a course of action based on the analysis while insisting on a certain predetermined outcome. A form of **responsibility outsourcing** similar to **responsibility escalation**.

Category

- Clear roles and responsibilities

Related patterns

- Real **strategy outsourcing** is so well-known as an antipattern that it happens only in the most clueless of organisations — if there is anyone in the management with half a clue, any strategy outsourcing is more likely to be a laundering.

IT Mismanagement Patterns

- **Apples from the tree** (or, better yet, several generations of them) can create an environment where strategy laundering and other responsibility avoidance tricks become the norm.

- Strategy laundering is sometimes used as an important insurance step before embarking on a **holy cow project** or a cycle of **management by hysteria**.

- The analysis produced by the external entity is useful as a way of **reverse requirements gathering**. This is somewhat similar

- In a situation of mature **runaway interdependence**, it is sometimes difficult and prohibitively expensive to analyse the baseline and take informed decisions on strategy; at the same time, no-one will allow you to make changes without analysis. Coming up with a green-field idea and resorting to strategy laundering to dissect this Gordian Knot[37] of bureaucracy and indirection may be the only way to bring about any change at all.

---

[37] The Gordian Knot is a legend associated with Alexander the Great. It is often used as a metaphor for an intractable problem (disentangling an "impossible" knot) solved easily by finding a loophole or thinking creatively.

Patterns

Strategy outsourcing

Hiring a consultant or a consulting company to take strategic decisions[38].

Granted, consulting companies know a lot about business in general, but unless you are really clueless, they do not know where *your* organisation needs to go better than you do. So when it comes to strategy, the management of the organisation should be the ones calling the shots. Strategy outsourcing also documents the absence of management vision which is highly problematic for working with both shareholders and the workforce.

---

[38]Note that sourcing of specific information and market research from consultancy companies is usually totally fine. To demonstrate the difference, asking a consultant "what are my competitors doing?" or "how many people would be interested if I am to offer product X?" is OK. Asking "what should we do?" is not.

Category

- Decision-making

Related patterns

- **Strategy laundering** is a superficially similar situation where the consultants are given specific guidance on the conclusions they need to produce.

- Not knowing, and having little time to learn the specifics of your business, the consultants are bound to produce general, standardised answers that will sound grand to management and hold well in court in case things go south. The resulting strategy, therefore, becomes the foundation block of **cargo cult standard compliance** even if the organisation was not already infested with it.

- When **news improvement** is practised in the organisation, the quality of input to the consultancy suffers from false claims about the current status. The consultant hired to develop a strategy has no means and no mandate to verify the input, so they have to hold it for true and inevitably produce a result with **critical dependency on imaginary assets**[39].

- Quality of input also suffers when any available **tainted knowledge** is not shared with the consultant.

- Outsourced strategies, like any measure taken without the participation of those who are affected by it, tend to lack support and feeling of ownership by staff. Their implementation, therefore, requires **pushers**.

---

[39]Indeed, the dependency is there even without the consultant, but the organisation may be habitually and instinctively avoiding its negative effects in internal operations. Consultants have no such option.

Patterns

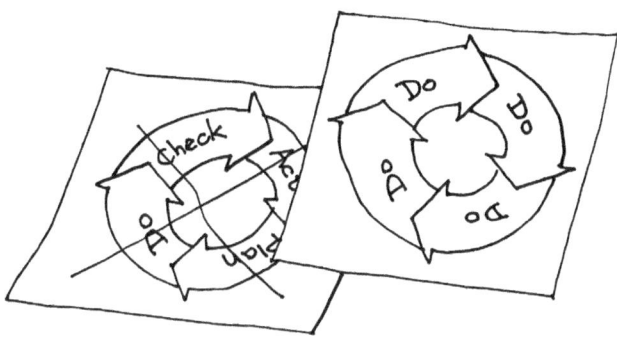

Submission to urgency

Perpetual reallocation of resources to what is considered the top priority at the moment due to impending deadlines or brass pressure. This is commonly done with no regard to the original intent and no plan for the use of the above-mentioned resources, thus causing further emergencies and schedule slips.

Category

- Planning

Related patterns

- Working on what is commonly recognised as the most urgent at the moment is good publicity whereas working on things that can wait may actually lead to trouble with the stakeholders of the more urgent need. Being so well received by others and so ineffective in achieving actual results, submission to urgency is a perfect method of **activity imitation**.

- Oxymoronic methods, such as the **avalanche model**, are commonly used to cover up and enable submission to urgency from the process side.

- Out of the three project management constraints, the schedule is the most visible one: when something is late, the higher-up notice it immediately. This makes submission to urgency a common tool in the middle managers' fight against **cast iron triangles**.

- As an alternative to sacrificing the schedule by submitting to urgency, the manager may elect to sacrifice scope and quality in a **quick fix of doom**.

Suboptimal improvement

Replacing a functioning system or procedure with another that is functionally inferior but more in line with some high-level strategy. It is usually hoped that the change will ultimately lead to a real improvement when the strategy, often dependent on a **wunderwaffe project** of some kind, is fully realised. Needless to say, this might take some time or never happen at all.

Category

- Business justification

Related patterns

- **Looking into the future** is the usual argument for suboptimal improvements.
- The **primacy of principles** is used to present suboptimal improvements as the right or only possible thing to do.

IT Mismanagement Patterns

- Suboptimal improvements create problems rather than solutions thus **fabricating business case** for further work.

- **God mode** and disregard for **tainted knowledge** inspire decision-makers to mandate suboptimal improvements, and **Einbahnstrassen** confirm and reinforce related decisions.

- Competent and engaged staff tend to rebel against suboptimal improvements, so they are usually delivered using a mix of **pushers** and **global zeros**.

- The most tear-jerking suboptimal improvements are those selected using a **lock, stock and barrel** approach and delivering only 80% where their predecessor delivered 100%. Bonus points if they are implemented to achieve **Potemkin standard compliance**.

Tainted knowledge

Failing to learn from successes of one's predecessors while building a new system that is supposed to be an improved version of some existing system. The designers of the new system view the old one as being inherently bad, so they refuse to even look at it while designing the replacement. This prevents them from learning about previously known solutions to problems that they will encounter.

Category

- Decision-making
- People

IT Mismanagement Patterns

Related patterns

- **Architectural answering machines** only appear to intentionally disregard tainted knowledge or have any opinion on it whatsoever. In reality, they have no intention to discuss anything — their job is to play back architectural guidance and let you speak after the beep.

- When **every change is sacred**, so are changes to things that already work well. Even if we succeeded last time, why not try to do things differently this time?

Patterns

Troglodyte manager

A manager who voluntarily limits his communication means in a way that only pleasant communications reach him, thus skewing his view of the business context. Such limitation of communication may take the form of ignoring e-mails from certain individuals, not turning up for meetings, pretending to be too busy to speak to selected visitors and callers and not being in the office when negative news is most likely to be delivered.

Category

- Communication
- People

Related patterns

- Becoming a troglodyte manager is a stepping stone to becoming a **manager in absentia**, the bottom of manager's potential well.

- **Einbahnstrasse** is naturally formed by a troglodyte manager's refusal to consider any feedback other than approval and support to his actions.

- Saying "no" is, invariably, a source of stress and negativity. So troglodyte managers are most likely to engage in **news improvement**, **deadline-driven estimations**, **faking ends meet** and declaring **umphs**.

Patterns

Turn into hedgehogs[40]

A superficially wise and correct decision or recommendation made without consideration for critically important details or the feasibility of its implementation in the business context. This is a typical product of **architectural answering machines**.

Category

- Decision-making
- Fact-based environment

---

[40]This refers to a joke about the mice who came to the wise owl to seek advice on how they could avoid being exterminated by the fox. The owl proposed that the mice turn into hedgehogs. The mice, extremely enthusiastic about the prospect, inquired about the possible means of such transmutation. The wise owl said: "You should figure out the details yourselves. I am a strategist!"

IT Mismanagement Patterns

Related patterns

- Project managers are sometimes implicitly expected to turn into hedgehogs by being placed inside **cast iron triangles** or being given **critical dependencies on imaginary assets** to manage.

- Every time the brave **McClanes** and watchful **guardian angels** protect their manager's behind, they increase the chance of being commanded to turn into hedgehogs in the future.

- The **primacy of principles** is a way of making turning into hedgehogs part of an organisation's culture.

Umph[41]

Formally declaring as delivered and closing an important project with a product that is unfit for purpose or altogether unusable. Umphs tend to happen when no measurable success criteria are defined before starting the work.

Category

- Fact-based environment
- Documentation and reporting

Related patterns

- An umph can provide a relatively simple exit from the cycle of **responsibility escalation**.

---

[41] When you triumph without trying.

IT Mismanagement Patterns

- Sufficiently entrenched **Einbahnstrassen** allow using umphs as a radical form of **news improvement**. If management is sufficiently isolated from the reality on the ground, it can be made to believe in the success of a project that has, in fact, failed.

Unbribe

Something other than a bribe that sways the decision-maker toward a course of action that directly benefits a certain party (the unbriber), and not the organisation whose interest the decision-maker is supposed to represent. An unbribe appears as if the decision-maker has been bribed by the benefiting party but, in reality, ignorance or laziness[42] on the part of the decision-maker is frequently the reason. Common examples of unbribery are covering up failures of contractors or preferential treatment of one vendor even though better options are available. In some cases (such as defining a policy that inadvertently favours a small group at a cost to the public interest), the decision-maker is not even aware that someone stands to benefit from a decision so unfairly that it would come across as a corrupt practice.

---

[42]This is reminiscent, as are many other patterns in this book, of Hanlon's Razor, a statement that one shouldn't assume malice when stupidity would suffice as explanation.

IT Mismanagement Patterns

Category

- Decision-making

Related patterns

- During cycles of **management by hysteria**, the decision-makers appear to grossly favour the vendor of the platform of choice (POC). They might not be actually bribed but merely unbribed.

- **Escalation of commitment** can be a powerful unbribe when external parties are involved in the strategy, the commitment to which is escalating.

- **Business case protectionism** frequently smells like corruption. In reality, the managers may have decided to reduce their worries to one **holy cow project** and not spend their feeling-important time and personal risk budget on anything else.

- Receiving kickbacks is the usual conspiracy theorist explanation for things the manager **bought before he thought**.

- For an outside observer, an unbribe is often indistinguishable from a bribe. Even in the absence of any criminal intent, it may still look shady enough to create an impression that feedback would be unwelcome, and thus lead to the **silence of the maltreated minds**.

Virtual support contract

A support contract, the main purpose of which is to ensure that the responsibility for any problem with the supported item lies with an external entity.

The availability of a support contract is often pitched as an important requirement when making technological choices. However, virtual support contracts are not intended to obtain actual support.

Category

- Business justification
- Clear roles and responsibilities

IT Mismanagement Patterns

Related patterns

- Those with **enterprise solutions** and protruded **beams in the eyes** like to point out unavailability of support contracts in otherwise perfectly supported free software.

- Support contracts that are maintained although they cannot be used effectively are elements of **cargo cult standard compliance**.

- Virtual support contracts, through **news improvement**, may be seen inside the organisation as something that can actually be relied upon, thus creating a risk of **critical dependency on imaginary assets**.

- Virtual support contracts are a form of **unbribery** — the contractor receives the payment without having to do much, but the decision-maker is motivated by their own concerns that have nothing to do with benefits to the contractor.

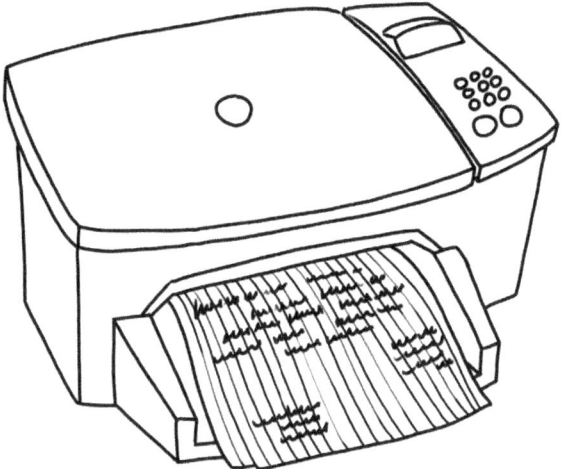

Write-only document

A document created to fulfil the requirement of a formal methodology, typically in the interest of **Potemkin standard compliance**. The content of such a document does not come close to the intended purpose dictated by the relevant standard, but the sign-offs are obtained anyway because the approvers are unwilling to read it before signing or not qualified to comprehend the content. Sloppy language and vaguely formulated commitments in write-only documents are typically abused and creatively interpreted *ex-post* to justify a project or service delivery manager's own decision-making beyond their normal authority or to provide an excuse for problems.

Category

- Documentation and reporting

IT Mismanagement Patterns

Other related patterns

- Write-only documentation can be useful as a sophisticated technique of **responsibility escalation**. Once approved, they can be used to demonstrate approval by senior management of any interpretation of the vagueness contained within.

- Write-only documents often create strong emotions in the unlucky reader. Before authoring or commissioning such documents, the creators should make sure they have achieved **silence of the maltreated minds** in the organisation or at least that all potential readers of the document are **global zeros**. On the other hand, **silence of the maltreated minds** might be a natural consequence of asking for feedback on long and meaningless documents.

- In organisations with **split personality order**, write-only documents occur naturally in the suppressed, but still functional, administrative structure.

Wunderwaffe[43] project

A project that is expected to produce great benefits via not very well understood means. A wunderwaffe project is often a figment of an incompetent manager's ego or a covert plan to secure a large budget and visibility for an activity that is not understood and thus cannot be easily measured or monitored. The scope of such projects is typically very large and fuzzy. There is also a tendency to further inflate it to make the results look even more impressive and justify the ever increasing amounts of time and resources required to achieve it. It is common to postpone other development activities, asserting that the wunderwaffe project will be able to provide the functionality or will allow developing it cheaper, faster and better.

---

[43] A (German) wonder-weapon. This term was invented and used by Dr. Joseph Göbbels and his Ministry of Public Enlightenment and Propaganda in Nazi Germany. Wundewaffe research was generously funded throughout the Nazi rule, and the progress, and any interim successes in the weapon's creation, received all possible publicity. However, none of the Wunderwaffe projects came to the point of effective use in the theatre of war before the fall of the regime.

IT Mismanagement Patterns

The wunderwaffe project thus experiences further scope creep and urgency boost.

Category

- Fact-based environment
- Documentation and reporting

Related patterns:

- Wunderwaffen flourish in organisations that use **publicity-based valuation** of projects.

- When a **wunderwaffe** project secures funding (but there's still no clarity about the actual plan), a copious amount of **activity imitation** is a common way to maintain the illusion of grandeur.

- The general fuzziness of the implementation plan in **wunderwaffe** projects often results in **critical dependencies on imaginary assets**.

- Wunderwaffe projects tend to turn into **holy cows** very early in their life cycle. It is more or less a requirement that they do so to sustain funding and management support for an activity that nobody really understands.

- To exit a **wunderwaffe** project, its leaders use various techniques of commitment de-escalation, such as **scope drain** and **umph**.

Categories

People love to classify things, the authors of this book are not an exception. We indulge in classification throughout the book as our mismanagement patterns are, essentially, a nomenclature of destructive behaviour. Why not go one step further and classify patterns themselves? Ta-da... enter the categories.

The categories listed below represent broad management topics. Heavy books and countless scientific papers have been written on each of them. In the coming few pages, we will not attempt to squeeze the present state of management science to any degree of detail. The goal of this chapter is to look at these topics from an engineer's perspective, point you towards important aspects, and structure your further thinking and searching for your own style and approach.

A list of patterns that belong to each category is located under the category description. You can use these as a list of examples of situations and behaviours that could be addressed with some of the recipes in the category description.

IT Mismanagement Patterns

Business justification

> *A true King would not waste time justifying or explaining. He would simply state his will.*
> Stephen King

Business justification is all about alignment of everything the organisation does or sponsors with its business objectives. Some would say that business justification is an easier subject in for-profit organisations, where the objective is to earn money and justification of any investment may be measured with some easily-calculated three-letter-acronym metric, like ROI[44]. Reality, as it happens, is more complex, as calculation of ROI expects "cost of investment" as one of the parameters, and figuring it out may be next to impossible with the complexity and uncertainties of modern

---

[44] Return on investment, the simplest of such metrics.

business. Indeed, if a highly reputable automobile manufacturer invests in software to trick hazardous emissions tests, they may turn good profits from this software for years. But if this is discovered the ensuing damage may ruin the whole business.

Business justification is often cursed in IT circles of organisations that consider themselves not to be "an IT organisation". In for-profits the powers-that-be look for the money, and if IT is nowhere to be found in the way these powers view the value chain, nothing IT does will ever produce money. Others will, enabled by IT, while IT remains the "way-too-expensive cost centre". In non-profits where the culture of business justification is much weaker, IT staff will often invoke business justification when objecting to another cosmetic improvement to a big boss's pet project. The same boss would turn down a much-needed security-related upgrade, citing lack of business justification as the reason.

Despite all the challenges, business justification remains a crucial way of understanding whether an initiative is worth doing, how it fares against alternatives and how important it is compared to other initiatives. It is also useful when business justification is formulated in a way that speaks to everyone in the organisation, from the executive level to the guy implementing the initiative by crawling under the server room's false flooring every day for a month. People feel better and work better when they know why they are doing what they have to do and agree with it.

A good business justification is usually one that can be expressed with numbers. Quantify required investments and your returns, preferably in terms of money or whatever you use to measure your success. Non-profits frequently have a particular challenge here. In fact, success of any non-profit mission may be quantified with one or more down-to-earth[45] indicators.

Figure out any alternatives or catastrophic risks related to undertaking (or not undertaking) the project. Alternatives need to be

---

[45] It is important for your quantifiable unit to be a matter of your immediate or next-to-immediate control. If you are an environmental NGO, the "number of people we convinced to consume less red meat" is a good one, but the "number of degrees we cooled the global atmospheric temperature" is not.

evaluated and quantified with the same accuracy and impartiality as your proposal. Catastrophic risks need to be clearly outlined: the attractiveness of a trip to Mars may be reduced by the fact that there is a 60% chance of dying before getting there and a 90% chance of never coming back.

As a quick start, try to answer the following questions:

- Is there any possibility at all that we'll fail our mission because we don't do this? Or because we do this?

- What is the expected benefit from undertaking this project (adjusted for all risks and uncertainties)? If your mission is primarily not about money, quantify it in relevant units.

- Is there anything we should do instead of this? In particular, is doing nothing[46] better than doing this?

The considerations of business justification apply not only to things specifically designated as "projects" but to everything done by the organisation, like purchasing a coffee machine for the office, standardising on a common platform for all websites, or conducting performance reviews. They also apply to the assessment of business justification itself. There seems to be an infinite cycle of "assessing the business justification of assessing the business justification of ...", and indeed there could be, if not for some observations that allow us to dodge the infinite recursion:

- If something is obviously not harmful and very cheap, and it's easier to do it than to assess if it's worth doing, we can just do it.

- What worked before will probably work again under similar circumstances. Learning from experience allows us to be more efficient in choosing the best thing to do.

---

[46] If you are wondering how that might be the case, think about your ability to take advantage of future opportunities. If you commit all your resources now and then a better opportunity comes along, with what resources will you be pursuing it?

- By the same token, what never worked before will only start to work if something has changed significantly in our environment and circumstances. Make sure you think of that when planning your next organisational restructuring.

Patterns in this category

- Activity imitation
- Analysis paralysis
- Architectural answering machine
- Business case fabrication
- Business case protectionism
- Common malpractice
- Cost sink
- Cutting the wrong corners
- Death march
- Enterprise technology
- Escalation of commitment
- Fake training
- Holy cow project
- Holy rodeo
- Management by hysteria
- Manualisation
- Pareto denial
- Publicity-based valuation

IT Mismanagement Patterns

- Responsibility escalation
- Reverse business justification
- Robin Hood financial management
- Suboptimal improvement
- Virtual support contract

Categories

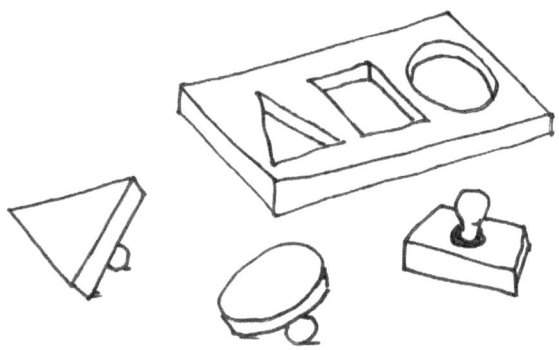

Clear roles and responsibilities

> *It is not only for what we do that we are held responsible, but also for what we do not do.*
> Moliere

It has likely occurred to anyone following the side-splitting and deeply thoughtful *Dilbert* comics by Scott Adams that Scott, in fact, has a spy in his own organisation. He doesn't. There is, simply, a limited number of distinguishable ways to screw up in management. Mapped to a much higher number of managerially challenged organisations, the blunders are doomed to reproduce in myriads of copies. The authors are aware of an organisation that grew concerned about the duplication of work and established teams to address the issue... *multiple* teams. It was a shock to then see a *Dilbert* strip about it because the situation appeared so unique in its pathetic-ness.

Anecdotes aside, having clear roles and responsibilities is important for many reasons other than avoiding redundancy. There are, fundamentally, four reasons to have a clear picture in this domain.

Firstly, "responsibility" means that somebody's softer part is on the line. It is useful for a manager to have a "securing my butt" frame of mind when thinking about distributing roles and responsibilities to his reports. Have you mapped all of the responsibility for your functional area to your subordinates? Do they know about it? Do they have the right tools and powers to deliver? Do you trust them to protect this precious part of your wobbly flesh? As a good manager, you will take responsibility for the team's performance, or deficit thereof, to the outside world; but for yourself, you need to know who covers each of the lunar zones. If you are all clothed and armoured by your stellar team — great! If you see that some of your backside is still bare — you know where to patch things up.

Secondly, sometimes it is difficult to find who is responsible. To make it much simpler, when you assign responsibility, assign it to one person. You cannot ask your "team" to deliver. You can ask Jane to deliver and inform John and Jack that Jane may use a certain amount of their time to help her with this task, and then provide any other necessary resources and authorities that Jane doesn't have the rank to obtain herself. You should also make sure that Jane knows she can revert to you if something goes wrong and she faces a problem that is above her pay grade. Only then will you be able to hold her accountable. The good news is you usually won't have to: given the sense of ownership of the task and everything necessary to do a good job, people get motivated and prepared to give their 120% to achieve the goal.

Thirdly, collective and outsourced decision-making are difficult to part with permanently. The temptation to share responsibility is natural, and if you have not been paying attention, your organisation already has a few committees with decision-making power, or has hired a consultant to make an important decision. Committees and experts are good for collecting different perspectives, brainstorming, discussing and debating, and creating as much decision-support information as possible. But making a decision is a lonely job and it is for the one responsible for the outcome, alone, to have the final word.

Finally, whether someone has succeeded or failed at their task is often far from obvious. Have they failed because of poor performance, because they were not given the essential resources, or because a catastrophic risk has materialised? Have they succeeded because of them and their team's great performance or as a side effect of somebody else's great performance? Or because of a windfall? When succeeding, have they exhausted the opportunities that presented themselves or relaxed immediately when the original expectations were formally met? When setting goals and assigning responsibility, define what success looks like as clearly (and as wisely) as possible.

Patterns in this category

- Circular decision
- Concealed consensus
- Goodbye party
- Guilt-based management
- Irrational unified process
- Local hero
- Manager in absentia
- Responsibility delegation
- Responsibility outsourcing
- Shadow governance
- Split personality order

IT Mismanagement Patterns

- Virtual strategy outsourcing
- Virtual support contract

Categories

Communication

> *The single biggest problem in communication is the illusion that it has taken place.*
> attributed to G. Bernard Shaw

How can we adequately stress the importance of this topic? Let's go with this: if you have to choose to care about just one of the categories, go for this one. Communication is the backbone of your organisational culture. The way you structure communication will have indirect but profound effects on how information is shared, how relationships are formed and how people work with each other. Waving communication issues away accumulates a "communication debt" with very high interest. In fact, it's not very uncommon for large and small organisations to go financially bankrupt in close succession to going bankrupt communication-wise.

As the wise author of the epigraph suggests, before improving communication it's better to make sure that object of planned improvement exists. The good news is that anyone can easily create communication where it doesn't exist. Sometimes, when communication has started, it feels like things were better without it. With very few exceptions, this is a wrong impression. Hold on to the communication line and improve from there.

IT Mismanagement Patterns

Shaping communication culture is a complex task. The biggest problem with it is that the effects of any interventions come weeks, sometimes months, later, so connecting them and excluding other influencing factors is practically impossible. Human brains are not set up to work with cause and effect so far apart in time, but with experience come the right intuitions about the course of action.

It is usually better to establish an open communication culture and nudge people towards it. There are situations when secrecy is necessary, but openness by default is a good option, unless you work for the CIA. It is particularly important that the feedback channels are open, easy to use and non-threatening. Better decisions can be reached when the decision-makers have a feeling for how their decisions are perceived.

Patterns in this category

- Assertion of culture
- Einbahnstrasse
- God mode
- Guardian angels
- Troglodyte manager

Decision-making

> *The whole problem with the world is that fools and fanatics are always so certain of themselves, and wiser people so full of doubts.*
> Bertrand Russell

Decision-making is simple in theory. Start with facts about the organisation and its environment, use the model of both to predict what will change in response to your actions, then chose the action that produces the best expected outcome given your goals, values and risk appetite. In practice, we don't know all the facts, the model is incomplete, the goals and values are rarely precise and we often don't have enough time for a complete analysis. Decision-making turns into a balancing act between choosing the best course of action and doing so before it's too late.

It is possible to speed up decision-making without sacrificing timeliness. For example, you can restructure the processes to make sure that decision-makers have the necessary information at their fingertips, so they have more time to analyse. You can also document past decisions and the reasons for them so that the thinking can be reused. Whatever you do, be mindful of the trade-off between timeliness and quality and make this choice consciously.

At the end of the day, with any process decisions are made by people. It used to be a matter of debate whether human choices are primarily rational or emotional, but the latest advances in the science of mind have brought an end to the controversy. For the most part, emotions and intuition reign supreme, and the rational mind is relegated to the role of producing rationalisations for our emotionally driven decisions[47]. We think this is not a reason for despair: despite being irrational, we managed to survive and build this civilisation with the Internet, airplanes and nuclear power plants. See this as a call to update the process:

- Learn about human biases and heuristics[48] and develop the emotional intelligence[49] and self-awareness to be able to identify them in your own thinking.

- Use formal methods, quantify amounts and probabilities, define the decision criteria and apply them. You might still choose to incorporate aesthetics or gut feeling as one of the parameters in the system, but be explicit about it.

- Show your analysis to someone who knows the substance area but has a different perspective, and ask them for feedback. Whether they agree with you or not, do not stop at confirming that and try to understand their reasoning.

- Involve others in the decision-making: groups of people are often more rational than individuals. The decision will usually take longer and cost more with a group, but it will be of

---

[47] *Quasi Rational Economics* by Richard Thaler gives a good overview of the role that emotions play in decision making, even with experts.

[48] For a serious reader interested in the subject, we recommend *Thinking Fast and Slow* by Daniel Kahneman.

[49] *Emotional Intelligence* by Daniel Goleman is a great read on this.

higher quality, especially if you ensure diversity of viewpoints and good moderation.

- When you involve others, it might be wise for them to do some independent thinking first, before being exposed to the others' ideas. This helps to mitigate groupthink.

- Better processes produce better decisions, but don't overdo it. Mature processes usually cost more. Is the better quality of this decision worth the price you'll have to pay for it? Is there a way to get the same quality cheaper?

Whether it be one person or a group, you still need to decide who will be making each decision. In some organisations everything is decided at the very top. Others give people complete independence. For most organisations the optimum will be somewhere in the middle. It is important that people have a say in decisions that affect them: not having a voice is very demotivating. Conversely, those who don't feel the effects of the decision will have little incentive to make a good one. In particular, take care with outsourcing important decisions to external entities. They might have the expertise but do they share your goals and values? Do they have enough skin in the game?

Making the decision is not the end of the process. If implementation takes some time, it might make sense to revise the decision when conditions change. This will be easy if all input to the decision process and the analysis that led to the outcome is documented. After the implementation is complete and the effects come into force, it's useful to look back and see if the analysis was correct. Some people say that changing decisions would put their leadership in question and that reviewing past mistakes creates regret and doubt. There may be some truth in this, but we think that the learning opportunity and the ability to correct course are more important.

Finally, both in the decision-making process, and in the decisions themselves, simple and proven options should be the default. Make sure you have good reasons before rejecting them. Thinking

IT Mismanagement Patterns

outside of the box is great, and sometimes necessary, but remember that this comes with associated costs and risks.

Patterns in this category

- Analysis paralysis
- Architectural answering machine
- Beam in the eye fallacy
- Buy before you think
- Circular decision
- Cutting the wrong corners
- Enterprise technology
- Every change is sacred
- God mode
- Lock, stock and barrel
- Management by hysteria
- McClane effect
- Primacy of principles
- Risk of programming
- Strategy outsourcing
- Tainted knowledge
- Turn into hedgehogs
- Unbribe

Documentation and reporting

> *Yes, man is mortal, but that would be only half the trouble. The worst of it is that he's sometimes unexpectedly mortal — there's the trick!*
> Mikhail Bulgakov,
> "The Master and Margarita"

The default way organisations store information is by putting it into people's heads. It's cheap, simple, time tested and requires no special arrangements. People remember things they work on, and in many cases that's enough. However, people get sick, they leave the company, forget and misremember, and sometimes disagree about what they have remembered. For critical information you need a more reliable type of memory, and this is where documentation comes in. Another reason to write documentation is to share knowledge with a wide audience: for a crowd over a certain size this becomes more efficient than addressing people individually.

Documentation can store information as long as you need and it can reach lots of people. This is a great power, but it doesn't come for free: documentation needs to be written, made available, catalogued and kept up to date. The standard rules of business justification apply to decisions of what documents to write. This is not about ticking the boxes — documentation must deliver value. The same applies to the content of each document; everything important should be in, clear and accessible, but once it is, the shorter the better.

It's useful to have documented guidelines for what should be documented and how. The guidelines depend on the size and the needs of the organisation so here we'll only go over the basics. First of all, document key decisions referencing their authors and justifications they used. Doing so establishes accountability and makes it easier to revise decisions later. If you're onboarding new people, you should have a friendly guide for the newbies to help them find their way around. Such a guide can be useful for the old guard too. Generally, if people ask you the same question more than five times, perhaps a piece of documentation is missing. After following this advice for a while, patterns start to emerge: capture them as valuable material for refining documentation defaults.

Once a document is written, you need to make sure that it can be found. We recommend having one entry point for all documentation, even if documents are physically stored in different systems and formats. Search is more important than having a taxonomy, but a good taxonomy is also helpful as it prevents duplication and facilitates explorative reading. Do not spend too much time designing the taxonomy though, growing it organically with periodic clean-ups is a good start and might be all you'll ever need.

The next question is access rights. For most organisations, giving read and write access to all members is a good default, but there will almost always be exceptions. Often, the exceptions apply to whole classes of documents and developing a policy for those special cases will save time spent on determining access rights at the document level. Writing the policy upfront might be a good idea if you already have experience, but it is more important to let it evolve according to the needs of the organisation.

For each document, it should be clear when it will be updated and who will do it. There are two options: plan a review at a specific time or outline the conditions under which the review should take place. The choice will be different for different documents: policies are often reviewed periodically while software documentation is usually updated in response to changes in the software. Having organisation-wide defaults is a good way to simplify the work of document authors and ensure consistency.

Another function of documents is giving an accurate and timely overview of the status and important events to people who make decisions. We call such documents "reports" and the process of writing them "reporting". To make reporting an effective means of communication, document any expectations: who creates the reports, using which medium, when and under which conditions, what they contain and who receives them. As with many things, having the process for adjusting reporting expectations is more important than getting the expectations right from the start.

Optimising the frequency and content of reports can be challenging: overloading decision-makers with trivial details impairs communication but so does delaying important news or missing important details. One promising approach in this area is "management by exception", whereby only deviations from a pre-approved plan are reported. This is not a silver bullet, however, as management by exception misses out on some motivational aspects of reporting and requires a certain level of process maturity — as well as professional maturity of all involved — to be reliable.

Patterns in this category

- Depreciation of commitment

IT Mismanagement Patterns

- Responsibility escalation
- Reverse requirements gathering
- Scope drain
- Umph
- Write-only document
- Wunderwaffe project

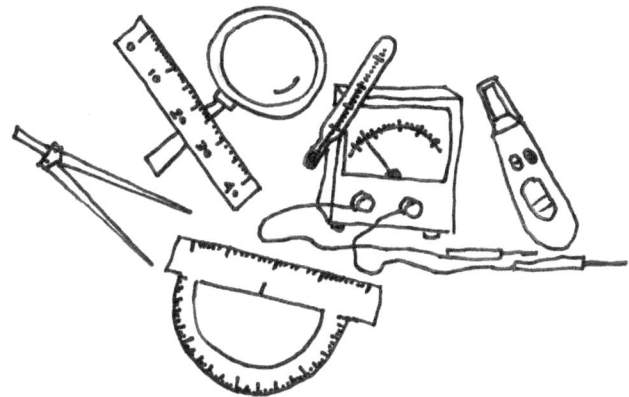

Fact-based environment

> *Two half-truths do not make a truth.*
> Artur Kösztler

You may be successful if you operate in total ignorance. If you take decisions without knowing anything, you may still get lucky. One should not underestimate the luck factor. Humanity's history is riddled with anecdotes of highly informed decisions that failed miserably because of bad luck. There is also a bunch of well-known nonsense decisions taken on an impulse that still led the decision-maker to a lucky triumph. Luck factor aside, the prospects of any decision tend to correlate positively with the amount of relevant accurate information at the decision-maker's disposal. A fact-based environment is a trait of an organisation's culture that simplifies decision-makers' access to relevant accurate information (facts) and minimises the influence of information noise (non-facts) and intentional deception (lies[50]).

The first major step in establishing a fact-based environment is the full empowerment of the "why" question. In fact, all non-trivial

---

[50] Call them "alternative facts" if you are a 2017 person.

decisions should be proactively equipped with fact-based justification by the decision-maker. Requesting justification of decisions should be allowed and encouraged, regardless of the requestor's rank and relationship to the decision in question. In some cases this will simply document such justification, which is useful for later analysis. Sometimes it will also provide important information to the requestor, which may be especially beneficial for junior staff who will use every opportunity to train their own decision-making apparatus. And sometimes it will actually challenge the decision-maker to think again and see if the justification is ripe for communication: rooted in data, free of emotions and transparent on where value judgement was used.

In fact, emotional, wishful and faith-based decisions are more common than people realise. It is important to test what you believe to be true if your decision hinges on whether it actually is. The fact that you really don't want something to happen doesn't make it less likely to happen. The converse is also true. Whether you are in a good mood today has no effect on facts. Strongly held beliefs and convictions are not facts: they may be based on irrelevant or outdated knowledge.

The good news here is that it is natural for human beings to challenge each other, and that their biases and beliefs may be different, especially in diverse teams that are more immune to groupthink[51]. Encourage discussion of observations and their interpretations in your team when you look for facts: facts will tend to be the statements that few want to challenge.

Last but not least, there must be ground rules on honesty. Lies, deceitful practices such as selective withholding of information, or intentionally proposing unlikely explanations when more likely ones are available, ruin the team spirit, dramatically affect the efficiency of the organisation and may lead to its untimely death. As stupid

---

[51]Groupthink exists in all groups. In homogenous groups, it is generally stronger and its nature is predictable. In diverse groups, individual biases cancel each other out and the effect of groupthink is weaker. At the same time, diverse groups tend to converge to a lower "common denominator" and are less capable of generating novel ideas.

Categories

as "zero tolerance" policies usually are, zero tolerance to dishonesty is one that actually makes sense.

Patterns in this category

- Confirmation-biased reporting
- Doomed to success
- Escalation of commitment
- Every change is sacred
- Faking ends meet
- Highlander principle
- Hope-based estimation
- Imaginary superpower
- Lock-in discount
- Looking into the future
- News improvement
- Potemkin standard compliance
- Primacy of principles
- Responsibility escalation
- Reverse requirements gathering
- Scale of economies
- Turn into hedgehogs
- Umph
- Wunderwaffe project

IT Mismanagement Patterns

People

Human beings are the quirkiest, the most unpredictable, the least reliable material we need to deal with in IT management. Their interests are not fully known even to themselves and they are guaranteed to be ill-aligned with the best interests of the company. People are dishonest about their motivations — oftentimes even with themselves. People get sick, infect others, have natural mood periods, form tribes, and engage in power struggles. If you look at your organisation as if it were a machine, good management is the lubricant and human nature is sand in the gears. If you can replace humans with robots and AI, do it and skip the rest of this chapter.

Humans are the most wonderful thing you will encounter in work life. They are creative, smart, passionate, compassionate, visionary, motivated and motivating. They are critical thinkers, rule-challengers, risk-takers, barrier breakers and achievers of the impossible. If you have not replaced your people with robots and you are still reading this text, things are not that bad! You can still make your organisation a well-tuned machine and have a great time and great learning experiences on the way there.

Myriads of studies and tonnes of books discuss how to manage people. Here is not a place to be comprehensive about this topic so we will go with the most important, basic guidance. People are different and have different needs. At the same time, it's possible to give general recommendations that are relevant for virtually everyone.

Do not offend or insult people. At differing levels, but dignity is important to everyone. Treat everyone with dignity and respect, especially those you suspect may be denigrating you or the organisation behind your back.

Generally, praise in public, criticise in private. Separate praise and censure, and do not "sandwich" critique between two flatteries: neither positive, nor negative comments will work if delivered this way.

Turn the culprit into an agent of improvement. When delivering critique, make sure to re-deliver the expectation that was not met, check understanding, and offer help and support. Do not push people to work against their nature: challenge them to become even better where they are already good.

Balance trust and verification. Not showing trust is considered by many as lack of respect or outright insult on their person. Showing trust may be a powerful motivator and loyalty-booster. At the same time, your people ought to feel that their work is going to be reviewed and evaluated by yourself, their peers, or others. It may happen sooner or later, but not too late to make them feel that it will never happen.

Perception of time varies a lot from one person to another. Observe how your people work with deadlines. Who is capable of managing a long deadline and produce a steady, stress-free stream of work? Who needs their work sliced more finely so they do not

IT Mismanagement Patterns

slack in the beginning and deliver late and sloppy work in the end? Who is stimulated by stress and works best when given tasks that are due "yesterday"?

The professionalism that we expect from staff includes distinguishing professional and personal. The problem with this, is that humans cannot evict their person from anything they do. Be caring and understanding of personal motives, but also set a clear line on how far you are prepared to go to accommodate your people.

People motivated by success are every manager's natural preference. Once hired though, such people need to be fed actual success from time to time to keep their spirits up. The first candidate here is of course work success: share all successes achieved collectively, speak about them a lot and acknowledge even the tiniest contributions. When there is no work-related success to be shared[52], share success in something else. As a team building exercise, do things that do not suck and are guaranteed to succeed. Cook or fish if you can guarantee success there. We are also not aware of cases of a team outing to a bar not succeeding.

Patterns in this category

- Disposable leader
- Doing other things
- Fake training
- Global zero
- Guardian angels
- Guilt-based management
- Local hero
- Manager in absentia

---

[52] Bad times for anyone and anything, including companies, are, generally, more certain than good times.

Categories

- Manager-in-the-middle attack
- McClane effect
- Pusher
- Runaway interdependence
- Shadow governance
- Silence of maltreated minds
- Tainted knowledge
- Troglodyte manager

IT Mismanagement Patterns

Planning

Adventure is just bad planning.
Roald Amundsen

Predicting the future is hard. Predicting how the future will change because of your actions is harder. The most predictable way through life is to decide to do something, do it immediately, analyse the effect, and only then proceed to the next thing. The more actions you plan at once, the longer in duration your plan is, the less certainty you can achieve in your planning. Still, humans like to plan and do lots of planning. Those who do *some* planning tend to be more successful than those who do *no* planning at all. However, the difference between those who do *some* planning and those who do *lots* of planning is much less pronounced. Indeed, it is also possible to ruin things with *too much* planning.

So, let's go with recommending that some planning is healthy. In order to be useful, your plan needs to be clear and realistic[53]. Let's look at these two concepts in more detail.

In order to be *clear*, your plan needs to talk about specific actions that have specific triggers. We will not go into detail on what specific actions are. Regarding triggers, it is good, but not mandatory, when such triggers are time-bound. "We'll do it at some point" is not a clear trigger, but "We'll do it when Jeremy has some spare time" might be.

In order to be *realistic*, your plan needs to be based on assumptions that are likely to work out. If you are planning to buy something, it's good to make sure that you can afford it. If you expect your staff member to do a barrel roll, he'd better have this ability on his resume. And if you need high-quality requirements to come from your client in a timely manner, this client would better have a track record of being such a unicorn.

"Clear and realistic" sounds simple but it is rarely achievable in real-life scenarios. Every time you have to compromise clarity or realism of your plan, record and track your risks.

Throughout this book, we preach ethics in management. We will walk a fine line right here and say that your sales pitch and your plan should not be the same thing. Indeed, you should not promise what you know you cannot deliver. At the same time, when you sell you speak to people's hearts and look for optimism. Your plan should be free of emotion and full of detail on risks and possible setbacks, including the ones that would scare the customer away from the deal.

The plan serves at least three purposes: it is a "to do" list, a vision of the future, and a contract between all of the plan's stakeholders. These purposes are in a conflict with each other, for example, the "contract" wants to stay unchanged and the "vision" wants to be updated. As your horizon advances, you obtain better information to hone the parts of the plan you were only able to roughly sketch before. We believe that change should prevail, but

---

[53]See also G.T. Doran's SMART criteria for objectives: `https://en.wikipedia.org/wiki/SMART_criteria`

IT Mismanagement Patterns

it is important keep the peace between stakeholders while implementing the change. A good tool for that is to have a pre-agreed and predictable change process that is fair to everyone's interests.

One situation that should definitely trigger an update of the plan is when something goes not as you assumed it would. As it can be tricky to assess (or even remember!) all the assumptions you had at the beginning of the project, a good approach is to establish tolerances on all relevant constraints (scope, schedule, budget, quality, resources and risks) from the outset and update the plan whenever you learn that at least one of them will be exceeded.

Finally, plans need to be communicated to others at every point in their lifetime. First off, nobody, not even you, has the full picture of reality: seek feedback on your plans from the widest possible audience. Once you are about to implement your plan, be discreet in how prominent you make it to your people in day-to-day work: some people thrive on having a longer-term perspective while others see it as stress factor and would much rather just do what you ask them to do today.

Patterns in this category

- Analysis paralysis
- Cast iron triangle
- Critical dependency on imaginary assets
- Deadline-driven estimation
- Death march
- Goodbye party
- Hope-based estimation
- Irrational unified process
- Late awakening

- Lock-in discount
- Quick fix of doom
- Scope drain
- Submission to urgency

IT Mismanagement Patterns

Recruitment

> *One cannot hire a hand;*
> *the whole man always comes with it.*
> Peter Drucker

Recruitment is about how you agree to pay for people from the street to become your constant concern and worry, bring you trouble with customers, your projects, and the law, complain about you to each other and, anonymously, on social media, make voodoo dolls of you, and constantly look for new ways of taking advantage of the organisation. The ones you recruit will also try to perpetuate your having to pay them by making themselves indispensable, seize each opportunity to ask for more money and benefits, and they will reserve, and eventually use, the right to walk out of your deal and leave you in the cold.

What could possibly compensate for all these troubles? Your ideal employee. What they look like may differ a lot from organisation to organisation. Your management style, the desired culture, the business area in which you are operating and your business model are all at play in defining who your ideal employee is and how to search for them. So we won't offer you universal recruitment advice but we will describe the axes along which you need to tune your recruitment process.

Hierarchical organisations will look for employees who can supervise and respond positively to direction that is supplied to them externally. They can still be creative self-starters but they should be prepared to seek approval for their initiative and tow the party line against what their creativity tells them. Flat organisations will look for employees with initiative and creativity, paired with enough self-discipline to keep their eyes on the ball without external control. The majority of people are more suited to hierarchical environments. At the same time, dreaming up innovation at work is more natural when you feel free to dream.

Staying on the topic of innovation, innovative and regulated areas may — and frequently do — coexist in one organisation. You would typically want an innovative person for a creative writing position and a rule-abiding one in accounting or quality control. Gauge the risk appetite of your applicant against what you consider appropriate in the position in question: for innovative positions you want risk-takers and rule-challengers whereas for regulated positions you want rule-abiding, patient and diligent people whose improvement initiatives will be guaranteed to stay within the limits set by existing rules.

Different types of people are required depending on whether they develop a product or provide a service. For products, you would typically select employees with engineering sharpness, intelligence, an unforgivingly critical eye and attention to detail. To provide services, you need "people people", with customer orientation, communication and persuasion skills, and emotional intelligence.

The present size of your organisation should also influence your recruitment strategy. In a small organisation, each new recruit is a major influencing factor for culture and interpersonal dynamics. Make sure you hire those who will bring along a positive change.

IT Mismanagement Patterns

In a larger organisation, new individuals do not influence the *status quo* as much so make sure they are compatible with the existing management system and rules, and won't create a major disruption.

The same considerations about influence on culture and internal dynamics apply when looking at the age of the organisation. Newer organisations are more vibrant and more susceptible to change their ways in the direction shown by one new charismatic individual, no matter how low their position is. Older organisations are likely to reject disruptors of their culture, so if you want to influence culture through recruitment, make sure that your new people also have the necessary diplomatic and persuasion skills to fit in.

You often hear that diversity is good for you — and we generally agree. At the same time, when it comes to recruitment, we have to qualify this statement. Any diversity relevant to performance and culture has to be taken into consideration in recruitment[54]. In a small and/or new organisation, you would, generally, want less diversity. Mono-cultured teams have more intrinsic trust, are faster, more united, and have minimal communication and understanding issues. They may be blind to specific issues and sources of information but, in a small team, the risks that result from such blindness usually cost less than the communication overheads that diversity may create. However, as the organisation grows, so does the cost of any catastrophic risks, and you want to have more diverse eyeballs on the task to notice every threat (and every opportunity) that emerges. It becomes increasingly hard to keep the team mono-cultured as it grows, because you basically run out of people with an ideal cultural fit and have to start sacrificing other relevant competencies to maintain the culture.

You need very different people depending on whether your organisation supports an open exchange of information or operates on a "need to know" or more restricted terms of information sharing. You probably don't want a person who would publish on

---

[54]Most countries impose legal restrictions on which information can be considered when making recruitment decisions. There are also moral considerations involved. Do not break the law and be kind to your fellow human beings.

his Facebook page a company document with "CONFIDENTIAL" classification written all over, in any case, but "need to know" is a mental mode of operation that not everyone is capable of. For example, as a manager in a media business, you will look at this axis completely differently when you are hiring a journalist versus an HR staffer.

Last but not least, you must look at how much cooperation you want from your staff and how much competition you find healthy. Modern organisations differ greatly on this axis from loving-kindness cooperative ones, with how much you have helped your fellow colleague firmly first on your performance review, to "up or out" systems where people are spending all the time they have left from being brilliant bathing their dear colleagues in shit. You probably want your developers on the cooperative side and salespeople on the competitive one, but it's best to not go to the extremes with either.

In general, understand what makes your organisation strong and seek people who reinforce that. And when you realise that the right people are way outside your budget, rethink your strategy rather than trying to make do with what you can afford.

Another important question is whom to involve in recruitment. People that are good at something are usually better at judging the competence of others in that area, and more generally, great employees will be better at distinguishing great hires from the not so great ones.

Patterns in this category

- Apple from the tree
- Assertion of culture

IT Mismanagement Patterns

- Global zero
- Local hero

Quality

> *The quality that can be defined is not the Absolute Quality.*
> Robert M. Pirsig
> "Zen and the Art of Motorcycle Maintenance"

As the epigraph suggests, attempts to exhaustively describe quality are generally futile. What we can do instead is mention some of the most important aspects of quality in IT management, as well as frequently forgotten ones.

Quality of a product is intimately connected to its purpose. The same shoe might be great for going out to dinner and very bad for going to the mountains. Understanding the relevant parameters and their desired values is critical to making quality judgements. To understand if something is good enough or not we can ask the following:

- What are the requirements? What is it that we actually want to have?

- What is the relative importance of each requirement? How much do we care about each of parameters of our goal?

- What are the tolerances along each requirement? How much are we prepared to forgo on each of the requirements and still call the result a success?

- Have we achieved the acceptable performance for all of the requirements? If so, have we achieved the optimal level with the resources we had?

The product's fitness for its intended purpose (which is the minimal level of quality) may have requirements on dimensions that are easy to overlook. For example, your product may have excellent functionality but lack in usability so badly that nobody will actually use it. Did you need to bother creating all the great functionality in this case?

Some dimensions of quality are commensurable with others: deficiencies in one may compensated by the abundance of another. For example, if you are building a car and you managed to exceed the original requirements of the engine power, it might be OK to relax the requirements of the maximum weight. Other dimensions can't be substituted by anything else: if your car won't pass the safety test, you can forget about using it on public roads.

In the world of quality, perfectionism and sloppiness are equally dangerous traits. Quality is continuous, your product can always be better and it can always be worse. Your task is to find the right mark for your product that you can achieve with your means and to the satisfaction of the user. Quality always comes at a price. At some point, increasing quality further stops making business sense, unless you are making a luxury item or very "enterprisey" software where "high cost" may be seen as a positive characteristic.

While product quality is important, caring about product quality alone makes your quality efforts transactional and specific to this product only. A clever way of increasing the quality of all of your future products and make achieving quality cheaper is to continuously work on the *process* quality. Process quality works as a multiplier to your product quality efforts in the final product quality. Remember though that multipliers happen to fall below 1, and a poor process may ruin the best efforts to assure product quality.

Quality is everybody's responsibility. Depending on your organisation, you may have people whose job description is built specifically around quality. "Tester" is probably the most abundant quality-centric function in the industry, but other functions that look at quality assurance and process quality are equally useful.

Patterns in this category

- Lock, stock and barrel
- Quantity assurance
- Quick fix of doom

Bibliography

[1] Adams, Scott *Thriving on Vague Objectives: a Dilbert Book*, Andrews McMeel Publishing, 2005

[2] Brooks, Frederick P. *The Mythical Man Month*, Addison-Wesley, 1975

[3] Daniels, Aubrey C. *Bringing out the Best in People: How to Apply the Astonishing Power of Positive Reinforcement*, McGraw-Hill, 2000

[4] Green, K.C. *Gunshow Comic: On Fire*, Website, 2013

[5] Hunt, Andrew, and David Thomas *The Pragmatic Programmer*, Addison-Wesley, 1999.

[6] Judge, Mike, director *Office Space*, Twentieth Century Fox, 1999.

[7] Kahneman, Daniel *Thinking, Fast and Slown*, Penguin, 2013.

[8] Lynn, Jonathan *The Complete Yes Prime Minister* BBC Books, 1997.

[9] Machiavelli, Niccolo *Machiavelli: the Prince* Cambridge University Press, 2019.

[10] Martin, Robert C. *Clean Architecture: a Craftsman's Guide to Software Structure and Design*, Robert C. Martin. Prentice Hall, 2018.

[11] Martin, Robert C., et al. *Clean Code: a Handbook of Agile Software Craftsmanship*, Pearson Education, 2009.

[12] McTiernan, John, director *Die Hard*, Twentieth Century Fox, 1988.

[13] Mulcahy, Russell, director *Highlander*, Twentieth Century Fox, 1999.

[14] Ohno, Taiichi. *Toyota Production System: beyond Large-Scale Production*, CRC Press, 2014.

[15] Peter, Laurence J., and Raymond H. Hull *The Peter Principle* Pan, 1976.

[16] Rainwater, J. H. *Herding Cats: a Primer for Programmers Who Lead Programmers* Apress, 2002.

[17] Ross, Jeanne W., et al. *Enterprise Architecture as Strategy: Creating a Foundation for Business Execution*, Harvard Business School Press.

[18] Thompson, Leigh L. *The Mind and Heart of the Negotiator* Prentice Hall, 2009.

[19] Yourdon, Edward *Death March*, Prentice Hall, 2014.

[20] The Holy Bible: King James Version. Hendrickson Bibles, 2011.

[21] *"Doom"* Id Software, 2003.

[22] *A Guide to the Project Management Body of Knowledge: (PMBOK® Guide)*, Project Management Institute, 2017.

[23] *Managing Successful Projects with PRINCE2*, TSO, 2017.

[24] *The TOGAF Standard, Version 9.2.*, Van Haren Publishing, 2018.

[25] *ITIL Practitioner Guidance*, TSO, 2016.

www.ingramcontent.com/pod-product-compliance
Lightning Source LLC
Chambersburg PA
CBHW071021240526

45469CB00006BD/2031